Drew Provan

# iPad

7th edition
covers all models of iPad with iOS 9

In easy steps is an imprint of In Easy Steps Limited
16 Hamilton Terrace · Holly Walk · Leamington Spa
Warwickshire · United Kingdom · CV32 4LY
www.ineasysteps.com

Seventh Edition

Notice of Liability
Every effort has been made to ensure that this book contains accurate
and current information. However, In Easy Steps Limited and the
author shall not be liable for any loss or damage suffered by readers
as a result of any information contained herein.

Trademarks
All trademarks are acknowledged as belonging to their respective
companies.

In Easy Steps Limited supports The Forest Stewardship Council (FSC),
the leading international forest certification organisation. All our titles
that are printed on Greenpeace approved FSC certified paper carry the
FSC logo.

MIX
Paper from
responsible sources
**FSC** C020837
www.fsc.org

Printed and bound in the United Kingdom

ISBN  978-1-84078-706-1

# Contents

# 1 Welcome to Your New iPad

*The iPad is a multimedia tablet like no other. Its rich graphics and seamless integration with the pre-installed apps make it perfect for work and play. Most tasks requiring a laptop can be carried out on the iPad (with its iOS 9 operating system), which is light, power-efficient, instantly-on and incredibly intuitive to use. It also has a huge number of third-party apps to expand its already impressive capabilities and performance.*

# Welcome to the iPad!

Congratulations on buying an iPad; a sophisticated multimedia tablet computer capable of playing music, dealing with emails, browsing the web, organizing your calendar and thousands of other applications! Or maybe you haven't bought an iPad yet, but are considering doing so. Let's look at what you can use the iPad for:

- Listening to music

- Recording and watching videos

- Taking photos

- Reading ebooks

- Browsing the web

- Emails, contacts and calendars

- Social networking

- FaceTime video chats, playing games, and much more

### Will it replace my laptop?

In some cases, yes; particularly with the iPad Pro, a 12-inch iPad that is capable of significant productivity tasks and also has its own physical keyboard (sold separately). If you mainly do web browsing, check emails and use social networking apps then the iPad Air or iPad Mini can easily replace your laptop. If, on the other hand, you use your laptop to generate PowerPoint slides or create complex documents, then the iPad Pro may be a better option in terms of a replacement device.

### What's missing from the iPad?

There are features found on laptops and desktops that are missing from the iPad. At present there is no:

- SD card slot.

- USB slots (though the Apple Camera Kit does have a 30-pin plug which has a USB socket at one end, but this is to connect your camera rather than attach other devices).

- Ability to access files and drag them around or drop into folders. You can get files on the iPad, but it's clunky and not very intuitive.

**Beware**

Depending on your needs, the iPad may not be a laptop replacement. Assess your needs carefully before buying one!

**Don't forget**

Apple's website (http://www.apple.com/support/ipad/using/) has lots of helpful tips on using the iPad.

![NEW]

The New icon pictured above indicates a new or enhanced feature introduced on the iPad with the latest version iOS 9.

# iPad Specifications

Since its introduction there are now several different generations of iPad, including the iPad Mini, which is smaller than both the original iPad and the larger iPad Pro. When considering which iPad is best for you, some of the specifications to consider are:

- **Processor**: This determines the speed at which the iPad operates and how quickly tasks are performed.

- **Storage**: This determines how much content you can store on your iPad. Across the iPad family, the range of storage is 16GB, 32GB, 64GB or 128GB.

- **Connectivity**: The options for this are Wi-Fi and 3G/4G connectivity for the internet, and Bluetooth for connecting to other devices over short distances. All models of iPad have Wi-Fi connectivity as standard.

- **Screen**: Look for an iPad with a Retina Display screen for the highest resolution and best clarity. This is an LED-backlit screen and is available on the iPad Pro, the iPad Air 2 (and later) and the iPad Mini 3 (and later).

- **Operating System**: The iPad Pro, the iPad Air and the iPad Mini all run on the iOS 9 operating system.

- **Battery Power**: This is the length of time the iPad can be used for general use such as surfing the web on Wi-Fi, watching video, or listening to music. All models offer approximately 10 hours of use in this way.

- **Input/Output**: The iPad Pro, the iPad Air and the iPad Mini have similar output/input options. These are a Lightning connector port (for charging), 3.5 mm stereo headphone minijack, built-in speaker, microphone and micro-SIM card tray (Wi-Fi and 4G model only).

- **Sensors**: These are used to access the amount of ambient light and also the orientation in which the iPad is being held. The sensors include an accelerometer, ambient light sensor and gyroscope.

- **TV and Video**: This determines how your iPad can be connected to a High Definition TV. This is done with AirPlay Mirroring, which lets you send what's on your iPad screen to an HDTV wirelessly with AppleTV.

The latest iPads, the iPad Air 2, the iPad Mini 4 and the iPad Pro, come with silver, space gray or gold back-panels.

If you have a fourth generation iPad (or later) then it'll come with the Lightning connector. You'll need to buy adapters to connect it to your "old" 30-pin accessories, such as TV, iPod dock, etc.

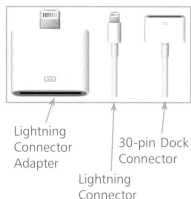

Lightning Connector Adapter

30-pin Dock Connector

Lightning Connector

# What's New in iOS 9?

iOS 9 is the latest version of the operating system for Apple's mobile devices including the iPad, the iPhone and the iPod Touch.

iOS 9 is an evolution of iOS 8, which followed iOS 7, one of the most dramatic cosmetic changes to the operating system in its history. It produced a flatter, cleaner design and this has been continued with iOS 9, which is not greatly different in appearance to its predecessor.

### Linking it all up

One of the features of iOS 9 is the way it links up with other Apple devices, whether it is something like an iPhone also using iOS 9, or an Apple desktop or laptop computer running the OS X El Capitan operating system. This works with apps such as Mail and Photos, so you can start an email on one device and finish it on another, or take a photo on one device and have it available on all other compatible Apple devices. Most of this is done through iCloud and once it is set up it takes care of most of these tasks automatically. (See pages 42-54 for details about setting up and using iCloud, the iCloud Drive and Family Sharing.)

### New and improved apps

iOS 9 comes with improved options for productivity, through the function of viewing more than one app on the screen at the same time (on certain models of iPad). There are also improvements to the Notes app so that lists can easily be created and photos added to notes. A new addition is the News app, which can display news items from a variety of organizations, covering a wide range of topics. The Music app now provides access to Apple Music, a new service that is the gateway to the entire iTunes music library. This is a subscription service, but there is a three-month free trial.

iOS 9 is a stylish and versatile operating system on the iPad and it also plays an important role in the holy grail of computing: linking desktop and mobile devices so that users can spend more time doing the things that matter to them, safe in the knowledge that their content will be backed up and available across multiple devices.

iOS 9, the latest version of the operating system used by iPads, can be used on all iPads from the iPad 2 (second generation) onwards and all versions of the iPad Mini.

iOS 9 for the iPad does not contain the Health app; this is just on the iPhone.

To check the version of the iOS, look in **Settings > General > Software Update**.

# Models and Sizes

Since its introduction in 2010, the iPad has evolved in both its size and specifications. It is now a family of devices, rather than a single size. When choosing your iPad, the first consideration is which size to select. There are three options:

- **Standard iPad**. This is the original size of the iPad. It measures 9.7 inches (diagonally) and has a high resolution Retina Display screen. The latest version, released in October 2014, is the iPad Air 2 which is the sixth generation of the standard-size iPads (updated with iOS 9 in September 2015).

- **iPad Mini**. The iPad Mini is similar in most respects to the larger version, including the Retina Display screen, except for its size. The screen is 7.9 inches (diagonally) and it is also slightly lighter. The latest version, released in September 2015, is the iPad Mini 4.

- **iPad Pro**. This is the latest size of the iPad to be introduced (announced in September 2015), and is aimed more as a replacement for laptop computers. It comes with a 12.9 inch screen. The iPad Pro can also be used with the Apple Pen stylus and the detachable Apple Smart Keyboard (both bought separately).

In terms of functionality there is little difference between the iPad Air and the iPad Mini, and the choice may depend on the size of screen that you prefer. Both the iPad Air 2 (and later) and the iPad Mini 3 (and later) have Touch ID functionality, whereby the Home button can be used as a fingerprint sensor for unlocking the iPad.

Another variation in the iPad family is how they connect to the internet and online services. There are two options:

- **With Wi-Fi connectivity**. This enables you to connect to the internet via a Wi-Fi router, either in your own home, or at a Wi-Fi hotspot.

- **With Wi-Fi and 4G connectivity (where available, but it also covers 3G)**. This should be considered if you will need to connect to the internet with a cellular connection when you are traveling away from home.

# Finding Your Way Around

The physical buttons and controls on the iPad are very simple. Additional functions, such as screen brightness, are software-controlled.

**Don't forget**

When you first unpack your iPad you will also find a Lightning/USB cable for charging the iPad or connecting it to a computer. There will also be a USB power adapter for charging the iPad. There is a range of iPad accessories available from the Apple Store, one of the most useful being a Smart Cover, for protecting the iPad and also putting it to sleep when not in use.

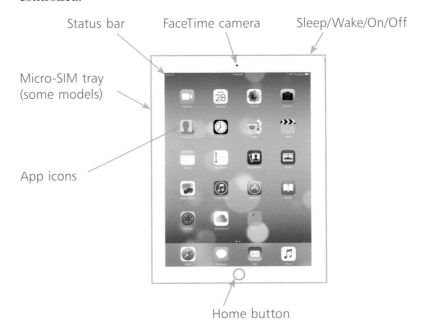

Status bar    FaceTime camera    Sleep/Wake/On/Off

Micro-SIM tray (some models)

App icons

Home button

**Don't forget**

The iPad Air 2 (and later) does not have a side switch, but all earlier models of the iPad and iPad Mini do. For models with a side switch, this can be used to mute the sound on the iPad, or lock rotation of the screen.

iSight camera    Microphone    Headset Jack

Side switch

Side switch

Side switch

Volume Up/ Down

Volume

iPad

Speaker    Lightning connector

The **network data icons** at the top of the screen are fairly similar to those found on the iPhone.

The fastest data connection is Wi-Fi. If no Wi-Fi is available you will need to use 3G/4G (if your iPad has this option) which is fairly fast. Unfortunately, as you move around, the 3G/4G signal will come and go so you may see the 3G/4G disappear and be replaced by the EDGE symbol (E). EDGE is slower than 3G/4G.

If you're *really* unlucky, the EDGE signal may vanish and you may see the GPRS symbol. GPRS is *very* slow!

| | | | |
|---|---|---|---|
| O | GPRS (slowest) | ◤ | Location services |
| E | EDGE | 🔒 | Lock |
| 3G | 3G | LTE | LTE |
| 4G | 4G | ⌬ | Personal Hotspot |
| ⌃ | Wi-Fi | ▶ | Play |
| ✳ | Bluetooth | ⊚ | Screen lock |
| ✈ | Airplane mode | ⟳ | Syncing |
| ✳ | iPad is busy | | |

The GPRS, EDGE and 3G/4G icons are seen on the models featuring both Wi-Fi and cellular only.

Don't forget

The iPad has many features which make it accessible to those with specific visual and audio needs. These features are covered in detail on pages 230-234.

You can see your active apps by bringing up the App Switcher window. If an app is misbehaving, quit it using the App Switcher window (see page 19).

To see the App Switcher window without having to press the Home Button twice, drag four fingers up the screen. You can also drag four fingers right or left across the screen to switch between open apps.

For more on swiping, tapping and pinching for getting around, see page 27.

# Home Button and Screen

There are very few actual physical buttons on the iPad but the Home button is an important one. The Home button performs a number of functions, including accessing the App Switcher window, where you can view your active apps and close them if required.

Home button functions:

- If you are on the Home screen (the first screen), press and hold the Home button to activate the Siri voice search assistant function.

- If you are on any other screen, press the Home button to go back to the Home screen: this saves you having to flick the screens to the left.

- When using the Music app, the Home button minimizes the Music window, allowing you to use other apps while listening to music.

- Pressing the Home button quickly twice brings up the App Switcher window (shows your active apps).

The **Home screen** is the first screen you see when you start up the iPad. It contains the apps installed by Apple, which cannot be deleted. In all, there are 24 of these – four will be on the Dock.

The Dock comes with four apps attached. You can move these off, add other apps (the Dock can hold a maximum of six apps or folders), or you can put your favorite apps there and remove those placed on the Dock by Apple.

You can move these apps to other screens if you want to but it's a good idea to keep the most important or most frequently-used apps on this screen.

The iBooks and Podcasts apps are now pre-installed on the iPad; in some previous versions of iOS they had to be downloaded separately, from the App Store.

By default there are four apps on the Dock at the bottom of the screen. You can add two more if needed. You can even drag folders to the Dock.

Network connections          Time          Battery

Wallpaper

Pre-installed apps          iPad screens          Apps on the Dock (up to 6)

To move an app, press and hold on it until it starts to jiggle. Then, drag it into a new position or onto the Dock. To move an app to another screen, press and hold on it and move it to the edge of the screen, until the next screen appears.

# App Switcher Window

The iPad can run several apps at once and these can be managed by the App Switcher window. This has been redesigned for iOS 9 and it performs a number of tasks:

- It shows open apps

- It enables you to move between open apps and open different ones

- It enables apps to be closed (see next page)

### Accessing App Switcher

The App Switcher option can be accessed from any screen on your iPad, as follows:

**1**   Double-click on the **Home** button

**2**   The currently-open apps are displayed, with their icons above them (except the Home screen). The most recently-used apps are shown first.

**3**   Swipe left and right to view the open apps. Tap on one to access it in full-screen size

# Closing Items

The iPad deals with open apps very efficiently. They do not interact with other apps, which increases security and also means that they can be left open in the background, without using up a significant amount of processing power, in a state of semi-hibernation until they are needed. Because of this, it is not essential to close apps when you move to something else. However, you may want to close apps if you feel you have too many open or if one stops working. To do this:

**1** Access the App Switcher window. The currently-open apps are displayed

**2** Press and hold on an app and swipe it to the top of the screen to close it. This does not remove it from the iPad and it can be opened again in the usual way

**3** The app is removed from its position in the App Switcher window

Don't forget

When you switch from one app to another, the first one stays open in the background. You can go back to it by accessing it from the App Switcher window or the Home screen.

# In the Control Center

The Control Center is a panel containing some of the most commonly used options within the **Settings** app. It can be accessed with one swipe and is an excellent function for when you do not want to go into Settings.

### Accessing the Control Center

The Control Center can be accessed from any screen within iOS 9 and it can also be accessed from the Lock Screen. To set this up:

**1** Tap on the **Settings** app

**Don't forget**

The Control Center cannot be disabled from being accessed from the Home screen.

**2** Tap on the **Control Center** option and drag the

**Access on Lock Screen** and **Access Within Apps** buttons On or Off, to specify if the Control Center can be accessed from there (if both are Off, it can still be accessed from any Home screen)

**3** Swipe up from the bottom of any screen to access the Control Center panel

**4** Tap on this button to hide the Control Center panel, or tap anywhere on the screen

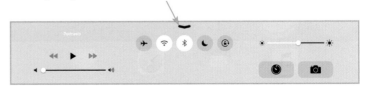

## Control Center controls

The items that can be used in the Control Center are:

**1** Use these controls for any music or video that is playing. Use the buttons to Pause/Play a track, go to the beginning or end and drag the slider to adjust the volume

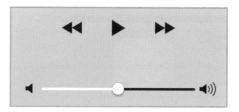

**2** Tap on this button to turn **Airplane mode** On or Off

**3** Tap on this button to turn **Wi-Fi** On or Off

**4** Tap on this button to turn **Bluetooth** On or Off

**5** Tap on this button to turn **Do Not Disturb** mode On or Off

**6** Tap on this button to access a clock, including a stopwatch

**7** Tap on this button to open the **Camera** app

**8** Use this slider to adjust the screen brightness

**9** Tap on this button to **Lock** or **Unlock** screen rotation. If it is locked, the screen will not change when you change the orientation of your iPad

*Hot tip*

The screen rotation can also be locked from within the **General** section of the **Settings** app. Under **Use Side Switch to**, tap on the **Lock Rotation** link, then the side switch can be used to lock, and unlock, the screen rotation. The iPad Air 2 (and later) does not have a side switch.

# Finding Things on the iPad

Sometimes you haven't got time to look through your entire calendar for an appointment, or to scroll through iTunes for one track. You can use Spotlight (Apple's indexing and search facility) to find specific apps, contacts, emails, appointments and music content.

### Start search

**1**  From any free area on the Home screen, press and hold and swipe downwards

**2**  You will be taken to the Spotlight Search screen

**3**  Enter your search word or string into the Search box

**4**  Your results will show up below. The results are grouped according to their type, i.e. Calendar appointment, email, etc.

# Finding Things with Siri

Siri is the iPad voice assistant that provides answers to a variety of questions by looking on your iPad and also at web services. You can ask Siri questions relating to the apps on your iPad and also general questions, such as weather conditions around the world, or sports results. To set up Siri:

**1** Open **Settings > General**, then tap on the **Siri** link

**2** Drag the **Siri** button to **On** to activate the Siri functionality

## Questioning Siri

Once you have set up Siri, you can start putting it to work with your queries. To do this:

**1** Hold down the **Home** button until the Siri window appears

**2** If you do not ask anything initially, Siri will prompt you with some suggestions (or tap on the **?** button in the bottom left-hand corner for more suggestions)

Some things you can ask me:

Play some blues

What films are playing?

How is the Nikkei doing?

Google the war of 1812

Set up a meeting at 9

Check my email

**3** Tap on the microphone button to ask a question of Siri

Hot tip

Turn **On** the **Allow "Hey Siri"** button in the Siri settings to activate Siri just by saying this, without having to press the Home button (when connected to power).

Don't forget

Within the Siri Settings you can select a language and a voice style.

23

Slide Over, Split View and Picture in Picture are also available on the iPad Pro.

# Multitasking on the iPad

The iPad has evolved from being an internet-enabled communication and entertainment device, into something that is now a genuine productivity device. With iOS 9, productivity options are expanded by being able to view more than one app at a time on the screen (only with certain models of iPad). This means that it can be easier to get tasks done, as you can see content from two apps at once.

## Slide Over

Slide Over is an option that is available on iPad Mini 2 (and later) and iPad Air (and later) and it enables you to access a bar of available apps. This is done by swiping inwards from the right-hand edge of the iPad screen. Tap on one of the apps in the bar to make it active in the right-hand side of the screen. Both of the windows can be used by tapping on them individually.

## Split View

On the iPad Air 2 (and later) the concept of Slide Over is taken one step further with Split View, when the second app is active in the right-hand side of the screen, drag the left-hand border of the app's window into the middle of the screen. Both open apps will now take up half of the screen and they can both be worked on independently of each other.

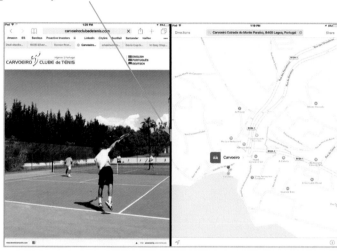

Swipe the button on the middle bar left or right to make either panel full-screen.

## Picture in Picture

The Picture in Picture function enables a FaceTime or YouTube video to be minimized on the screen, but remain active so that you can still view and perform other tasks at the same time.

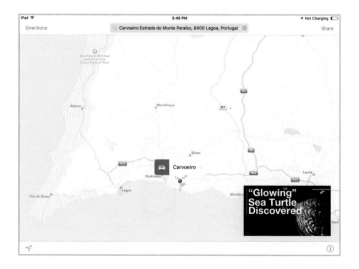

# Default Applications

These are some of the most popular pre-installed apps:

 **Calendar**: keeps your appointments in sync with your other Apple devices, using iCloud

 **Contacts**: lists all contacts including phone numbers, email, postal addresses and notes

 **Notes**: for jotting things down. Store notes within iCloud so that they are available on other devices

 **Maps**: GPS-enabled maps help you get from A to B, current position, and other information

 **Videos**: play movies and other video content, purchased or from your own collection

 **iTunes Store**: browse and buy music, movies, TV shows and more

 **App Store**: your central store for paid and free apps

 **Reminders**: to-do lists, sync with Apple Mail and Outlook Tasks

 **Messages**: send SMS-type messages free with Wi-Fi to other compatible devices

 **Settings**: this is where you make changes to personalize your iPad

 **Safari**: Apple's home-grown web browser

 **Mail**: handles IMAP and POP3 email, and syncs to your main accounts on your computer

 **Photos**: show your photos with slideshows, print off photos or share via Facebook, Twitter, etc.

 **Music**: controls music and provides access to the Apple Music subscription service

 **Game Center**: social gaming, lets you play games and interact with friends

 **Camera**: shoot stills or movies using front or back cameras similar to iPhone functionality

 **FaceTime**: video chat to others using iPad, iPhone or Mac

 **Photo Booth**: take still images and select from a series of special effects

 **News**: collates news content from numerous sources (not yet available in all locations)

 **Clock**: provides time in any part of the world. Useful as an alarm clock and a stopwatch

The News app is new to iOS 9.

# The Display and Keyboard

So, what's so exciting about the screen? What makes it so special? Firstly, it has a high quality Retina Display.

The technology behind the multitouch screen is ingenious. Using one, two, three or four fingers you can do lots of different things on the iPad, depending on the app you're using and what you want to do. The main actions are tap, flick, pinch/spread and drag.

The screen is designed to be used with fingers – the skin on glass contact is required (if you tap using your nail you will find it won't work). There are styluses you can buy for the iPad but for full functionality, fingers on screen give the best results.

| | |
|---|---|
| **Tap** | Apps open when you tap their icons. Within apps you can select photos, music, web links and many other functions. The tap is similar to a single click with a mouse on the computer |
| **Flick** | You can flick through lists like Contacts, Songs, or anywhere there's a long list. Place your finger on the screen and quickly flick up and down and the list scrolls rapidly up and down |
| **Pinch/spread** | The iPad screen responds to two fingers placed on its surface. To reduce the size of a photo or web page in Safari place two fingers on the screen and bring them together. To enlarge the image or web page spread your fingers apart and the image grows in size |
| **Drag** | You can drag web pages and maps around if you are unable to see the edges. Simply place your finger on the screen and keep it there but move the image or web page around until you can see the hidden areas |

Beware

The screen responds best to skin contact. Avoid using pens or other items to tap the screen. However, the iPad Pro does come with its own dedicated stylus: the Apple Pen (bought separately).

Hot tip

Use four fingers to bring up the App Switcher window (drag four fingers up the screen), or flick right or left using four fingers to switch between running apps.

## ...cont'd

**Don't forget**

The iPad Pro is designed to work with the Apple Smart Keyboard (sold separately).

The iPad is different to a laptop since there is no physical keyboard. Instead, you type by tapping the **virtual keyboard** on the iPad screen itself. You can use the keyboard in portrait or landscape modes. The landscape version provides much wider keys.

### The keyboard seems to change in different apps

The keyboard is smart – and should match the app you're in. For example, if you are word processing or entering regular text you will see a standard keyboard. But if you are using a browser or are prompted to enter an email address, you will see a modified keyboard with *.com* and @ symbols prominently displayed.

**Hot tip**

If you have Wi-Fi, try using your voice to dictate emails and other text using the Dictate option (its icon is on the left of the spacebar).

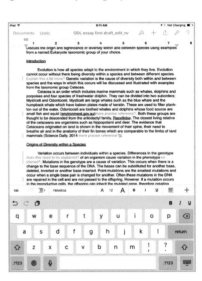

Top left: portrait keyboard in Mail

Top right: portrait keyboard in Pages

Bottom left: portrait keyboard in Safari – note the **Return** key has now changed to **Go**. Tap this to search the web or go to a specific URL

If you find you are making lots of typing errors, try switching the iPad to landscape mode (keys are larger).

Mail with iPad in the landscape position. Notice how wide the keys have become, making it easier to type without hitting two keys at once! Also notice the Dictation icon to the left of the spacebar (you get this when connected to Wi-Fi).

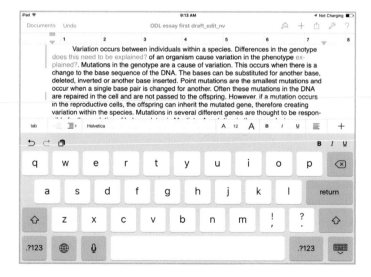

Pages with landscape keyboard. Again, the keyboard is large, but the downside is that you lose real estate for work – the effective area for viewing content is quite small. Dictation is active – you can tell because the icon has enlarged and shows the volume level as you dictate your text.

# Caps Lock and Auto-Correct

It's annoying when you want to type something entirely in uppercase letters, since you have to press Shift for every letter – or do you? Actually, there's a setting which will activate Caps Lock but you need to activate this in Settings:

 Go to **Settings**

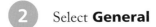 Select **General**

 Select **Keyboard**

4 Make sure the **Enable Caps Lock** slider is set to **On**

5 While you are there, make sure the other settings are on, for example the **"."** **Shortcut** (see below)

## Other settings for the keyboard

- **Auto-Correction** suggests the correct word. If it annoys you, switch it off.

- **Auto-Capitalization** is great for putting capitals in names.

- The **"."** **Shortcut** types a period every time you hit the spacebar twice. This saves time when typing long emails but if you prefer not to use this, switch it off. Here's another neat trick – you can also insert a period by tapping the spacebar with two fingers simultaneously.

**Hot tip**

If you do not like the default iPad keyboard, you can download other third-party virtual ones from the App Store. Three to look at are: SwiftKey, Swype and KuaiBoard.

As you type words, the iPad **Auto-Correct** will suggest words intelligently which will speed up your typing.

## To accept iPad suggestion

When the suggested word pops up, simply tap the space bar and it will be inserted. The suggested word may not be what you want, in which case you can reject it by tapping the 'x' next to the suggested word.

Don't forget

## To reject suggestion

Above the keyboard is the Shortcuts bar. This contains the **Undo** and **Redo** buttons and the **Paste** button for copied text. When you are entering text, the **Bold**, **Italic** and **Underline** buttons are also available in some apps, as is an option for adding photos or attachments.

Above left: the iPad will suggest a word but if you don't want to use the suggestion tap the 'x' next to it. The word you type will be added to your user dictionary.
Above right: You can look up the dictionary: tap the word twice, tap the right arrow and choose **Define**.

All contact names are automatically added to your user dictionary.

# Can I Use a Real Keyboard?

There are times when you need real physical keys. For example, if you are typing a longer document you might find tapping out your text on the glass screen annoying. Apple has designed a dock with an integrated keyboard, which is great for holding your iPad at the correct angle, and allowing your iPad to be charged while you type using the keyboard.

Original Apple iPad keyboard and dock

ZAGG proplus keyboard for iPad 2 (works with later models too)

The iPad Pro can be used with the Apple Smart Keyboard (sold separately).

For some older keyboards you will need the Lightning to 30-pin Adapter.

If you need to type long documents consider using a physical keyboard.

### Can I use a Bluetooth keyboard?

Absolutely! The iPad has Bluetooth built-in so you can hook up an Apple Bluetooth keyboard and type away. Alternatively, there are third-party keyboards such as the ZAGG proplus Bluetooth keyboard (**www.zagg.com**) which acts as a case when not in use (protects the front of the iPad but not the back).

# Keyboard Tricks

Although it's not immediately obvious, the keyboard can generate accents, acutes, and many other foreign characters and symbols.

Holding the letters "a", "e", "i", "o" or "u" generates lots of variants. Just slide your finger along till you reach the one you want and it will be inserted into the document.

For accents and other additional characters, touch the key then slide your finger to the character you want to use.

Also, when you use Safari you don't have to enter ".com" , ".co.uk" , etc. in URLs – the **?** key will produce other endings if you touch and hold the key.

# Select, Copy and Paste Text

Rather than retype text, you can select text (or pictures) and paste these into other documents or the URL field in Safari. Touch and hold text, images or URL (links) to open, save or copy them.

### To select text

Touch and hold a paragraph of text to select. Drag the handles to enclose the text you want to copy then tap **Copy**.

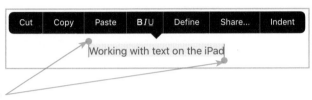

Copy web links by tapping and selecting **Copy**. If you just want to go to the website, click **Open in New Tab**.

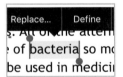

Use the built-in dictionary by tapping a word then **Define**.

Paste copied text or images by tapping the screen in Pages, for example, and tapping on the **Paste** button.

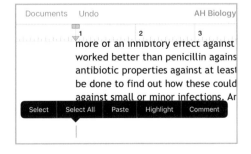

# Editing Text

Once text has been entered it can be selected, copied, cut and pasted. Depending on the app being used, the text can also be formatted, such as with a word processing app.

## Selecting text

To select text and perform tasks on it:

**1** To change the insertion point, tap and hold until the magnifying glass appears

**2** Drag the magnifying glass to move the insertion point

**3** Tap once at the insertion point to access the menu buttons

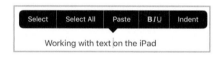

**4** Double-tap on a word to select it. Tap once on one of the menu buttons as required

**5** Drag the selection handles to expand or contract the selection

**6** Use the Shortcuts bar on the keyboard to, from left to right, cut the selection, copy the selection, or paste the selection

# Using Predictive Text

Predictive text tries to guess what you are typing and also predicts the next word following the one you have just typed. It was developed primarily for text messaging and it can now be used on the iPad with iOS 9. To do this:

**Don't forget**

If Predictive is Off in Step 3, the QuickType bar does not appear above the keyboard. You can also toggle predictive text On or Off by pressing on this button on the keyboard and tapping the Predictive button On or Off.

**Don't forget**

Predictive text learns from your writing style as you write, and so gets more accurate at predicting words. It can also recognize a change in style for different apps, such as Mail and Messages.

**1** Tap on the **General** tab in the Settings app

**2** Tap on the **Keyboard** option

**3** Drag the **Predictive** button **On**

Predictive

**4** When predictive text is activated, the QuickType bar is displayed above the

keyboard. Initially, this has a suggestion for the first word to include. Tap on a word or start typing

**5** As you type, suggestions appear. Tap on one to accept it. Tap on the word within the

quotation marks to accept exactly what you have typed

**6** After you have typed a word, a suggestion for the next word

appears. Tap on it to use it, or ignore it if you wish

# 2 Getting Started

*As with most technology, although the iPad is plug-and-play, there is some initial setting up to do. It's worth spending some time setting up the iPad so it best suits your needs.*

# Turn On and Off

You can put your iPad fully off, or into sleep mode (sleep mode is useful because as soon as you press the Home button the iPad is instantly on).

- If the iPad is fully off, press and hold the **On/Off** button – the iPad will start up.

- When you have finished using it, simply press the **On/Off** button briefly and the iPad will enter sleep mode.

- Sleep mode uses very little power so for the sake of speed, simply use sleep mode unless you are not going to use the iPad for several days.

- To wake from sleep, press the **Home** button or **On/Off** button.

- The Lock Screen will be displayed. Swipe the **slide to unlock** option to the right to access the Home screen.

Use sleep mode to turn your iPad off unless you are not planning to use it for an extended period.

You can configure the Side Switch to lock the screen in portrait or landscape mode by choosing **General settings > Use Side Switch to: Lock Rotation or Mute**. (The Side Switch is not available on the iPad Air 2 and later).

**38**

**...cont'd**

## To fully power off

**1** Press and hold the **On/Off** button until you see the slider bar and **Slide to Power Off** appears

**2** Slide the red slider to the right

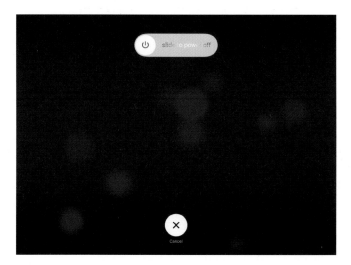

As with the other screens on the iPad, the Lock Screen can be displayed in portrait or landscape mode.

**3** The iPad will fully shut down

## Lock the screen

The iPad works in portrait (upright) and landscape (sideways) modes. The iPad is clever and can tell which way up it is being held and the screen will rotate accordingly. Sometimes you will want it to stay fixed in portrait or landscape modes. This can be done with the Screen Lock function. This can be controlled using the Control Center. To do this, swipe up from the bottom of the screen and tap on this button.

# Syncing with iTunes

The iPad and iOS 9 are both very much linked to the online world, and the iCloud service can be used to store and synchronize several types of content. However, it is still possible to use iTunes on a Mac or PC to sync content, including:

- Music

- Videos

- Apps

- TV shows

- Podcast

- Books

iTunes can be used so that you can sync these items (or some of them) onto your iPad. To do this:

**Don't forget**

In some previous versions of iOS, other types of content could be synced with iTunes, such as Notes and Calendars. However, these can now all be saved, stored and synced in iCloud. See pages 42-49 for more detailed information about iCloud.

**1** Connect your iPad to your computer. iTunes should open automatically but if it does not, launch it in the usual way. Click on your iPad at the top left-hand corner of the iTunes window. Click on the **Summary** tab to view general details about your iPad

**2** iTunes can also be used to back up your iPad (in addition to iCloud). To do this, click on the **This computer** button under the **Automatically Back Up** section or click on the **Back Up Now** button

**3** Click on the categories in the left-hand panel to select the items that you want to sync. These include Apps, Music, Movies, TV Shows, Podcasts, Books, Audiobooks and Photos

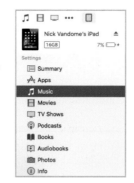

**4** Select what you want to sync for each heading (this can be for items in a category or selected items)

When you are syncing items to your iPad it is best to select specific folders or files, rather than including everything. This is because items such as music, videos and photos can take up a lot of storage space on your iPad if you sync a large library from your computer.

**5** Click on the **Apply** button to start the sync process and copy the selected items to your iPad

**6** On the **Summary** page in Step 1, scroll down to view the options for syncing, such as specifying only checked songs and videos to be synced, or manually manage your videos for syncing

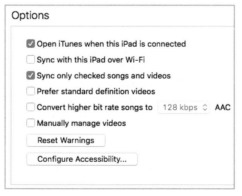

41

# Using iCloud

iCloud is a service that allows you to use the cloud to sync your data (Calendars, Contacts, Mail, Safari bookmarks, and Notes) wirelessly.

Once you are registered and set up, any entries or deletions to Calendars and other apps are reflected in all devices using iCloud.

An Apple ID is required for using iCloud, and this can be obtained online at **https://appleid.apple.com/** or you can create an Apple ID when you first access an app on your iPad that requires this for use. It is free to create an Apple ID and requires a username and password. Once you have created an Apple ID you can then use the full range of iCloud services.

### iCloud settings

Once you have set up your iCloud account you can then apply settings for how it works. Once you have done this, you will not have to worry about it again:

**1** Access the **iCloud** section in the Settings app

**2** Drag these buttons to **On** for each item that you wish to be synced with iCloud. Each item is then saved and stored in the iCloud and made available to your other iCloud-enabled devices

The iPad apps that require an Apple ID to access their full functionality include: iTunes Store, Messages, iBooks, FaceTime and the App Store.

...cont'd

## Using iCloud online

Once you have created an Apple ID you will automatically have an iCloud account. This can be used to sync your data from your iPad and you can also access your content online from the iCloud website at **www.icloud.com**

1 Enter your Apple ID details

2 The full range of iCloud apps is displayed, including those for Pages, Numbers and Keynote

> **Don't forget**
>
> When you register for iCloud you automatically create an iCloud email account, which can be used on your iPad and also online.

3 Click on an app to view its details. If iCloud is set up on your iPad, any changes made here will be displayed in the online app too

## Find my iPad

This is a great feature which allows you to see where your devices are. Once activated (**Settings > iCloud > Find My iPad**), sign in to iCloud using a web browser on any computer and click Find My iPhone. This will find your iPad and any other devices you have registered.

> **Hot tip**
>
> iCloud provides 5GB free storage but you can pay for more (*correct at the time of printing*).

43

# About the iCloud Drive

One of the options in the iCloud section is for the iCloud Drive. This can be used to store documents so that you can use them on any other Apple devices that you have, such as an iPhone or a MacBook. To set up iCloud Drive:

**1** In the iCloud section of the Settings app, tap on the **iCloud Drive** option

**2** Tap on the **iCloud Drive** button so that it is **On**

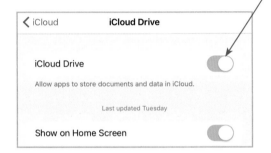

Some third-party apps are compatible with the iCloud Drive, but the standard ones are some of Apple's own apps, such as Pages, Mail, Numbers and Keynote.

**3** Once the iCloud Drive has been activated, tap on any listed apps so that they can sync with iCloud Drive

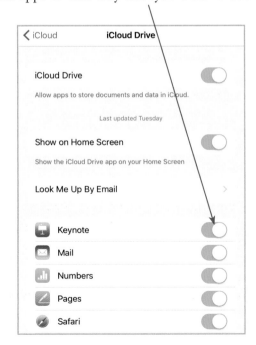

**4** When you are using an app that has iCloud Drive capabilities it may ask you to turn on iCloud Drive for the specific app, if it has not already been done. Tap on the **OK** button and open the Settings app

**5** In the Settings app, open the settings for the specific app (in this case, Pages) and drag the **Use iCloud** button to **On**. Any document created, or edited, by this app will automatically be stored in the iCloud Drive

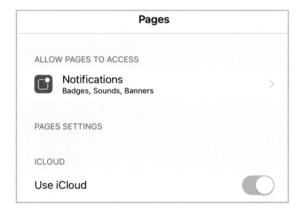

To access documents on iCloud Drive on other devices, these devices need to have iCloud Drive turned On and activated for the required apps.

45

**6** The documents in the app on your iPad can be viewed on your other Apple devices if you have iCloud turned on and iCloud Drive activated. For iOS 9 devices they can be viewed from the Documents section of the compatible apps (such as Pages, Numbers and Keynote); for OS X Yosemite (and later) devices they can be viewed in the iCloud Drive section in the Finder

# Using the iCloud Drive App

Once the iCloud Drive has been set up, files that are stored there can be viewed using the iCloud Drive app and items can be added to the iCloud Drive from individual apps. To use the iCloud Drive app to view files:

Some of the folders in Step 2 may be those that have been created within the iCloud Drive on other devices, e.g. a MacBook.

**1** Tap on the **iCloud Drive** app

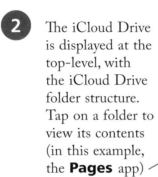

**2** The iCloud Drive is displayed at the top-level, with the iCloud Drive folder structure. Tap on a folder to view its contents (in this example, the **Pages** app)

**3** The contents of the folder are displayed. Tap on an item to view it

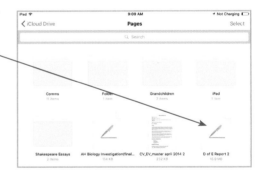

**4** Documents can be viewed from within the iCloud Drive app but they cannot be edited since it is not their native app. However, they can be shared and copied to their native app by tapping on the **Share** button

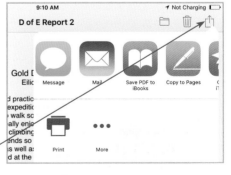

## Adding items to the iCloud Drive

If compatible apps have been set up for the iCloud Drive (see pages 44-45) then they can be used to create documents, which will automatically be saved to the iCloud Drive. To do this:

**1** Open an app (in this example, Pages) and tap on the **Create Document** button

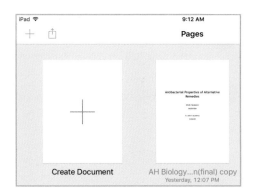

**Don't forget**

Once the iCloud Drive has been set up, documents will be saved there automatically.

**2** Create the new document. It will be added within the app

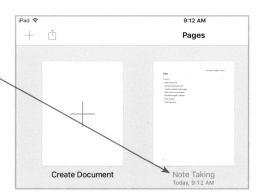

**3** In the iCloud Drive app the newly created document is visible and it can be opened to view its content. It will also be available via the iCloud Drive on other compatible Apple devices and also the online iCloud Drive (see next two pages)

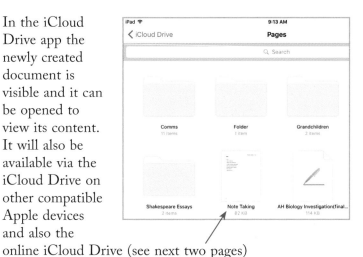

# Using iCloud Drive Online

Files that have been saved to your iCloud Drive on your iPad can also be accessed on any other Apple devices you have, such as an iPhone or a MacBook. They can also be accessed from your online iCloud account at **www.icloud.com**, from any internet-enabled computer. To do this:

**1** Log in to your iCloud account and click on the iCloud Drive button on the Homepage

**2** Your iCloud Drive folders are displayed. Click on a folder to view its contents

**Hot tip**

Pages, Numbers and Keynote can also open files created in the equivalent Microsoft Office apps, e.g. Word, Excel and PowerPoint.

**3** Content created with the relevant apps on your iPad will automatically be stored in the appropriate folders, i.e. Pages documents in the Pages folder, etc.

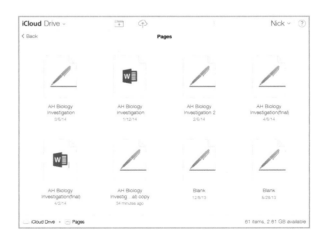

**4** Within a folder, use the buttons at the top of the window to, from left to right, create a new folder, upload a file from your computer, download a selected item from the iCloud Drive to your computer, delete a selected item or email it to someone

**5** From the Homepage of the online iCloud website, select one of the apps that use iCloud Drive, e.g. Pages, Numbers or Keynote

The available apps on the online iCloud website are only the Apple ones (Pages, Numbers, Keynote etc.), not any third-party ones.

**6** Create a document with the appropriate app. This will then be available on your iPad, using the equivalent app

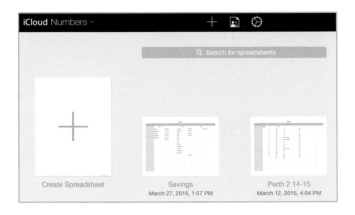

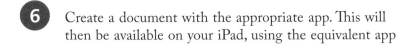

# About Family Sharing

As everyone gets more and more digital devices, it is becoming increasingly important to be able to share content with other people, particularly family members. In iOS 9, the Family Sharing function enables you to share items that you have downloaded from the App Store, such as music and movies, with up to six other family members, as long as they have an Apple Account. Once this has been set up, it is also possible to share items such as family calendars, photos and even see where family members are located, using Maps. To set up and start using Family Sharing:

**1** Access the iCloud section within the Settings app, as shown on page 42

**2** Tap on the **Set Up Family Sharing** link

**3** Tap on the **Get Started** button

**Don't forget**

You must have a valid form of payment for your Apple Account if you are going to allow other family members to buy content through Family Sharing.

**4** One person will be the organizer of Family Sharing, i.e. in charge of it, and if you set it up then it will be you. Tap on the **Continue** button (the Family Sharing account will then be linked to your Apple ID)

**5** Tap on the **Continue** button again

**6** If you are the organizer of Family Sharing, payments for items will be taken from the credit/debit card that you registered when you set up your Apple ID. Tap on the **Continue** button to confirm this

**7** Once Family Sharing has been created, return to the iCloud section in the Settings app and tap on the **Add Family Member** link

**8** Enter the name or email address of a family member and tap on the **Next** button

**9** An invitation is sent to the selected person. They have to accept this before they can participate in Family Sharing

Each family member has to have an Apple ID to join Family Sharing. If you are adding a child you can create an Apple ID for them at this point, if they do not have one.

Each family member has to be added separately to Family Sharing.

# Using Family Sharing

Once you have set up Family Sharing and added family members, you can start sharing a selection of items.

### Sharing Photos

Photos can be shared with Family Sharing thanks to the Family album that is created automatically within the Photos app, in the Shared section. To use this:

**1**   Tap on the **Photos** app

**2**   Tap the **Shared** button

**3**   The **Family** album is already available in the **Shared** section. Tap on the cloud button to access the album and start adding photos to it

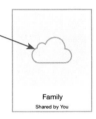

**4**   Tap on this button to add photos to the album

**5**   Tap on the photos you want to add and tap on the **Done** button

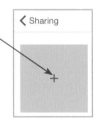

**6**   Make sure the **Family** album is selected as the Shared Album and tap on the **Post** button

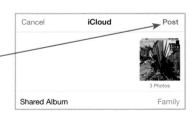

**Beware**

iCloud Photo Sharing has to be turned On to enable Family Sharing (**Settings > Photos & Camera > iCloud Photo Sharing**).

**Hot tip**

When someone else in your Family Sharing circle adds a photo to the Family album, you are notified in the Notification Center and also by a red notification on the Photos app.

## Sharing Calendars

Family Sharing also generates a Family calendar that can be used by all Family Sharing members:

**1** Tap on the **Calendar** app

**2** Tap the **Calendars** button to view the Family calendar

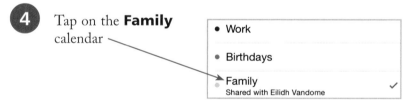

**3** Press and hold on a date to create a New Event. The current calendar will probably not be the Family one. Tap on the calendar to change it

For a more on calendars and creating events, see Chapter Nine.

**4** Tap on the **Family** calendar

**5** The **Family** calendar is now the active one

**6** Complete the details for the event. It will be added to your calendar, with the Family tag. Other people in your Family Sharing circle will have this event added to their Family calendar too and they will be sent a notification

53

Beware

Family Sharing can be set up so that individuals have to gain permission from the sharing administrator to buy their own items from the App Store or iTunes Store. This is usually for children when they do not have a credit card registered with their Apple ID.

Hot tip

The Find My iPhone app can be used in a similar way to Find My Friends and it can be used to find any lost or stolen devices belonging to members of the Family Sharing group.

**...cont'd**

### Sharing Music, Movies and Books

Family Sharing can also be used to share items such as apps, music, movies and books between members of the group. This can be done on mobile devices or desktop or laptop Apple computers. To access items from another Family Sharing member:

**1** Open the **iTunes Store** app (or the **iBooks** app of the **App Store** app)

**2** Tap on the **Purchased** button

**3** Tap on the iCloud icon next to an item to download it to your own device

### Sharing Locations

Family Sharing makes it easy to keep in touch with the rest of the family and see exactly where they are. This can be done with the Find My Friends app. The other person has to have their iPad (or other Apple device) turned on and online. To find family members:

**1** Open the **App Store** app and download the **Find My Friends** app

**2** A map is displayed with the location of any active and online members of the Family Sharing group

# Getting the iPad Online

The iPad is a fun device for listening to music, watching videos and playing games, but to experience the full potential you need to get it online.

## Getting online

The fastest connection is Wi-Fi. All iPad models include the Wi-Fi receiver which means you can browse available wireless networks, choose one and connect.

**1** Select **Settings > Wi-Fi**

**2** Slide the Wi-Fi slider to **On** if it is **Off**

**3** A list of available wireless networks will appear under **Choose a Network.** Tap the one you want to connect to

**4** You will likely be prompted for a username and password since most networks are locked (if the network is *open* you will get straight on)

**5** Check the signal strength indicator which will give you an idea of how strong the signal is

## Join networks automatically

If this setting is selected, your iPad will connect automatically to wireless networks. This is useful if you move from place to place and have previously joined their network – you will not be prompted each time to re-enter your details. But if you don't want the iPad to join networks automatically, switch this off.

Sometimes you don't want the iPad to remember all used networks (hotels, airports, etc.).

**1** Go to **Settings > Wi-Fi** and the select the network you want the iPad to forget

**2** Click the right arrow

**3** Tap **Forget this Network** and it will be deleted from the list

For a more detailed look at connecting with Wi-Fi see pages 71-72 in Chapter Three.

The iPad may join networks that you don't particularly want to join. Tell it to forget certain networks.

# The Pre-installed Apps

### App Store

This is the workhorse app on the iPad and gives you access to the online store where you can find thousands more apps to download, covering 24 different categories. (See page 186.)

The **Clock** and **Camera** are also classified as pre-installed apps: these both can be used to do what you would expect; tell the time in a variety of formats and locations, and take photos.

### Calendar

This app keeps you organized. It is similar to Calendar on the Mac and Outlook on the PC. The interface is beautiful and it's very easy to enter your appointment details. Usefully, the app's icon shows the current date before you click it to open the app. The Calendar app will be explored more fully in Chapter Nine.

The Calendar app's icon will show today's date even before you launch it, which is very useful.

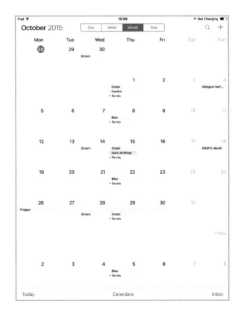

**...cont'd**

## Contacts
This app stores the details of all your contacts. Contacts resembles a physical address book with left- and right-facing pages.

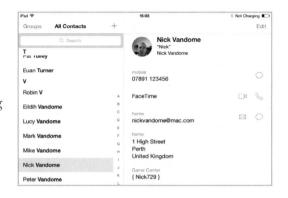

The app works in both portrait and landscape modes.

You can view contacts, add, edit and delete. If you want to add a photo to a contact this is very easy.

Contacts has smooth integration with Address Book on the Mac and Outlook on the PC. (See Chapter Ten.)

## Notification Center
As well as messages popping up on your screen from Facebook, iMessages, etc. you can also see all your notifications including anniversaries and other appointments using the Notification screen. From any screen, simply swipe your finger down the screen and all your notifications will appear.

Although the Notification Center itself is not a pre-installed app as such, it takes information from other apps such as Calendar and Reminders.

...cont'd

## Mail

Mail is the powerhouse for managing all of your email. The Mail app can handle multiple accounts, POP3, IMAP and Exchange (see page 95). The emails are easy to read and HTML is handled well. The app's views vary depending on whether you hold the iPad in portrait or landscape modes.

Mail closely resembles Mail on the Mac. (See Chapter Five.)

Some people say they prefer non-HTML email, but HTML email looks much nicer than plain email.

## Messages

This is the iPad app for sending text and photo messages (iMessages). In iOS 9 it is also possible to include video and audio clips and also send someone your location on a map. (See pages 103-104.)

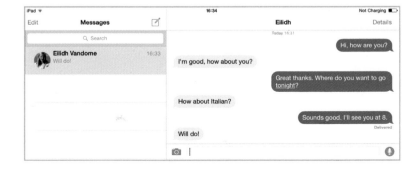

## Notes

This is very similar to Notes on the iPhone and Mac OS X. You can scroll through a list of notes, add new notes, edit, and share using email. You can also sync your notes from the iPad with the Mac and PC using the online iCloud service, if you have an account.

If you find Notes too limiting you can always view the huge variety of third-party apps on the App Store, or you could try a web-based notes service such as Remember The Milk (**rememberthemilk.com**) or Google Tasks. (See Chapter Eleven.)

## News

This is a new app in iOS 9 which collates news stories from publications which you specify, and then displays them together in the For You section of the app. (See pages 133-134.)

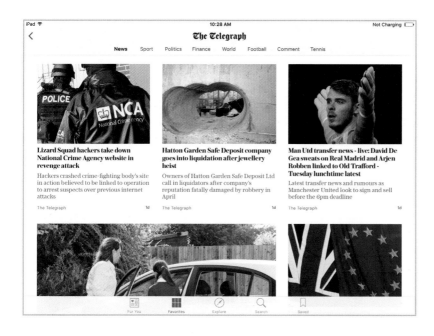

At the time of printing, the News app is only available in the US, the UK and Australia. It is gradually being rolled out to other regions.

**...cont'd**

### Videos

The iPad is a gorgeous multimedia device. Its large, high-resolution screen makes videos a joy to watch using the Videos app.

You can watch music videos and movies, rented or bought, from iTunes or you can copy your own movies across. Plug in a decent pair of headphones and immerse yourself!

Getting your own movies onto the iPad is very easy. (See Chapter Seven.)

### iBooks

This is now a pre-installed app on the iPad and it can be used to store your electronic books, and also browse the online iBook store for new titles to download and read. (See Chapter Sixteen.)

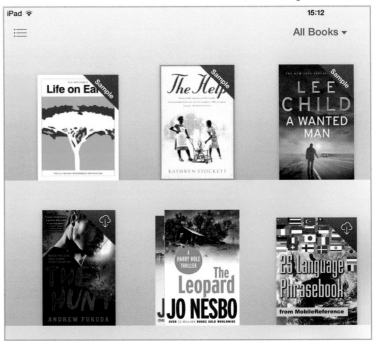

### Reminders

The Reminders app on iOS devices is a welcome addition. The interface is simple and easy to use. Reminders is also available as part of OS X Yosemite and later, and can sync both Mac and iOS devices such as the iPad.

### Game Center

For all gaming fans, this app can be used to download and play games from the App Store, play against other people in multi-player games and also compare your scores and achievements with other players.

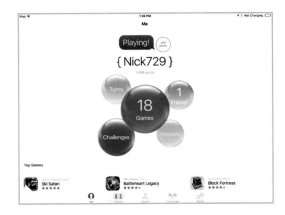

### Maps

The Maps app can be used for a variety of uses including looking up locations and destinations, finding directions, locating the addresses of contacts and viewing areas in 3D relief. (See Chapter Twelve.)

The **Settings** app allows you to customize the iPad to suit your specific needs.

...cont'd

## Settings app

The Settings app is the central hub for controlling all aspects of your iPad. It is the equivalent to System Preferences on your Mac or the Control Panel on the PC. We will explore this in greater detail in Chapter Three.

Use **Settings** for items including:

- Activating Airplane mode

- Connecting to Wi-Fi

- Setting notifications for individual apps

- Reviewing cellular data usage

- Adjusting the brightness of the screen, and choosing wallpaper

- Setting up Mail, Calendars and Contacts

- Controlling audio, Music, Safari

- Configuring FaceTime

## Safari

Although you can download third-party browsers from the App Store, Safari is the pre-installed browser on the iPad. It is fast, clean and easy to use. It is very similar to its big brother on the Mac and PC.

You can open several browser windows at the same time and toggle between them.

## Bookmarks

You can keep these in sync with Safari on your computer using either iCloud or iTunes.

Safari has an Address Bar/Search box for Google which you can switch to Yahoo! or Bing if you prefer. (See Chapter Four.)

If you don't want Google as your search engine – change it to Yahoo! or Bing. Go to **Settings > Safari** and specify your preferred search engine.

63

**...cont'd**

### Photos

Visually stunning, the Photos app is perfect for showing off your photos. You can review by Photos or Albums and play slideshows. There is also an option to share specific photos. (See Chapter Six.)

### iTunes Store

A selection of content, such as music, movies, TV shows and books can be downloaded using the iTunes Store app. (See Chapter Fourteen.)

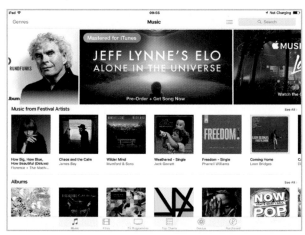

## Music

The Music app on the iPad is very similar to the conventional iPod but because the screen real estate is so large, you can view albums and their covers at a larger size, in all their glory! The layout of the screens is very clear, and you can select your music from Playlists, Albums, Artists and several other ways. It also provides access to the Apple Music subscription service. (See pages 170-174.)

## Podcasts

This is another app that previously had to be downloaded from the App Store but is now pre-installed. It enables you to search for and download audio and video podcasts on a range of topics. (See pages 135-136.)

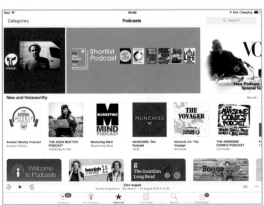

By using Playlists in the Music app you can gain complete control over your music library.

65

**...cont'd**

### FaceTime

Video chatting is a very personal and interactive way to keep in touch with family and friends around the world. The FaceTime app provides this facility with other iPad, iPhone and iPod Touch users, or a Mac computer with FaceTime. To use FaceTime for video chatting:

### What do you need?

**1**  iPad with FaceTime and a Wi-Fi or cellular connection

**2**  The other person needs FaceTime on their iPhone, iPad, or Mac. They also need to be on a Wi-Fi or cellular network

**3**  Apple ID (i.e. iTunes account, iCloud)

### Using FaceTime

**1**  Launch **FaceTime**

**2**  **Sign in** if not already signed in (you don't need to do this each time)

**3**  Tap **Contacts** and find the person you want to FaceTime chat with

**4**  Tap their **email address** or cell phone number (the latter will start a FaceTime call using their iPhone)

**5**  Add to Favorites if you plan to call this person regularly

**6**  Tap a contact in the **Video** tab to return a recent FaceTime call

## Photo Booth

As the name suggests, this app lets you take photos of yourself as if you were in a Photo Booth. It also has several built-in effects which distort the image.

**1** Launch **Photo Booth**

**2** Choose the effect you want to use, e.g. Thermal Camera, X-ray etc. If you want a standard image choose Normal

**3** Tap the **Shutter button** at the bottom and the Photo Booth will take a picture which will be added to your Camera Roll

## Tips

This app offers a range of help and advice about using the iPad and the apps that are on it. The tips are updated on a regular basis, so it is always worth looking at this app from time to time.

# Restore and Reset the iPad

If you are connected to iCloud, your entire iPad contents will be backed up every time you are connected to Wi-Fi.

If the iPad misbehaves, you can reset it and restore it from the iCloud backup. (You can also do this via iTunes if you have backed up your iPad here too.)

### Resetting the iPad

There are various options for resetting and restoring your iPad. These are accessed from **Settings > General > Reset**.

For all of the Reset options there is a confirmation window that needs to be actioned after you have tapped on a specific reset option.

**1** Click on the **Reset All Settings** option to return any settings you have applied to their factory defaults. No data or media is deleted with this option

| ‹ General | **Reset** |
|---|---|
| Reset All Settings | |
| Erase All Content and Settings | |
| Reset Network Settings | |
| Reset Keyboard Dictionary | |
| Reset Home Screen Layout | |
| Reset Location & Privacy | |

Use the **Reset Home Screen Layout** option to return the Home Screen to its factory settings.

**2** Click on the **Erase All Content and Settings** option to remove everything on your iPad and return it to its factory settings (only do this if you are sure it is backed up). This will erase everything on the iPad

### To restore the iPad

If an iPad has been reset with the **Erase All Content and Settings** option, it can be restored when it is turned back on. Select the option for restoring the iPad from the iCloud backup, rather than setting it up as a new device. You will have to enter your Apple ID with which you created your iCloud account, and the iPad will then be restored with the latest backup that was created in iCloud.

If you are selling your iPad, or giving it to someone else, make sure that you use **Erase All Content and Settings** before you hand it over. The new user will then be able to set it up as a new device or from their own iCloud backup.

# 3 iPad Settings

*The whole look and feel of the iPad is controlled through Settings, one of the apps pre-installed on the iPad. In this chapter we will look at all settings, from wallpapers to the Music app, getting things set up perfectly for optimal use.*

# Up in the Air

The iPad is a great multimedia device for listening to music or watching movies on the plane. There are strict rules about wireless and cellular receivers, though – these must be switched off during the flight. Airplane Mode switches all iPad radios off. Airplane Mode is only seen with the combined Wi-Fi and cellular models.

Turn on Airplane Mode when you fly! This turns all wireless transmitters and receivers off.

 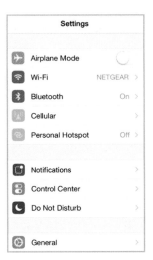

Settings on Wi-Fi model          Settings on Wi-Fi + cellular model

## Wi-Fi only models

Although the new iPad supports 4G, this functionality is not available in every country.

**1** Go to **Settings > Wi-Fi**. Turn Wi-Fi **Off** by tapping the **On/Off** button or sliding the slider to the right

**2** Wi-Fi is now fully off. You cannot receive Wi-Fi signals and the iPad is safe to use on the plane

## Wi-Fi and cellular models

**1** Go to **Settings > Airplane Mode** and push the slider to the right

**2** Wi-Fi and cellular radios are now fully off

For both models, when you are off the plane, go back to settings and slide the slider to the left which switches the radios back on.

# Getting Online with Wi-Fi

The iPad is designed to be used online – using either a wireless connection or cellular network. You can use it without internet access but you won't be able to browse online content, download apps, content, or update your apps.

## Connect to a wireless network

**1** Open **Settings > Wi-Fi**

**2** Make sure Wi-Fi is set to **On**

**3** Choose a network: you will see a list of available networks near you. If locked (most are) you will see a padlock symbol. Some networks may appear "open" and let you connect but when you browse you will be presented with a request for a username and password

**4** Tap the name of the network you want to connect to

**5** Enter the password if you know it

**6** You should see a check mark next to the network name showing which wireless network you have joined

**7** If your network is hidden but you know its name tap **Other...**

**8** You can allow the iPad to join networks quietly without alerting you (**Ask to Join Networks – Off**) or you may prefer to be asked before the iPad joins a network (**Ask to Join Networks – On**)

No Wi-Fi connection? If you have an iPhone, switch on **Personal Hotspot** (**Settings > Personal Hotspot**). This lets the iPad use the iPhone's cellular connection. Be careful – the data used comes out of your iPhone allowance!

**...cont'd**

**9** You can see the strength of the connection by checking the wireless icon at the top left of the iPad display or in the wireless connection window (in **Settings**)

### Setting network connection manually

**1** Tap the blue **i** symbol to the right of the network name

**2** You can choose an IP Address using **DHCP**, **BootIP**, or **Static Address**. **Subnet Mask**, **Router**, **DNS**, and **Search Domains** are also shown in the window though you won't need to change these

**3** If you use a proxy to get onto the internet, enter the details manually or set to **Auto**. Most people don't use proxies so it is unlikely you'll need to change anything here

There is another network setting for switching Bluetooth on or off, for sharing content over short distances with radio connectivity.

# Setting Up Notifications

If you have used the iPhone you will be familiar with notifications. These are audio and visual alerts used by some apps. For example, if you use a messaging app you may want to see how many unread messages there are without actually opening the app. Or, if you use an app like Skype, you may want to be shown on screen when someone is calling you even when the iPad screen is locked. By setting up your notifications you can choose how much or how little information you receive in terms of messages, calls, updates, etc.

### Set up notifications

**1**    Open **Settings > Notifications**

**2**    Under the **Notifications Style** heading you will see a list of apps that use Notifications

**3**    To configure Notifications for an app, tap its name in the list. You can then turn On or Off the **Allow Notifications** option and set a sound and style for how these notifications appear in the Notification Center

Spend some time setting up your **Notifications** to avoid unwanted intrusions from apps sending useless alerts!

Some apps offer notification by **Sounds**, **Alerts** and **Badges**. Sounds **On** means the iPad will play a sound when a notification is received. Alerts are messages that display on the screen, and Badges are the red circles that appear at the top right of the app's icon when notifications have been received.

If you want to keep intrusion from notifications to a minimum, you can adjust the settings on an app-by-app basis.

# Cellular Data

This is only shown in the combined Wi-Fi and cellular model.

### Check cellular data

 Go to **Settings** > **Cellular**

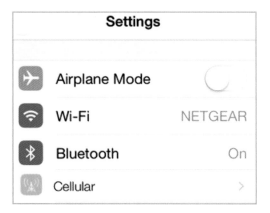

| Settings | |
|---|---|
| ✈ Airplane Mode | ○ |
| 📶 Wi-Fi | NETGEAR |
| ✳ Bluetooth | On |
| 📡 Cellular | > |

**Beware**

When abroad, keep Data Roaming Off or your phone bill may be huge – the cost of data download outside your own country is generally very high. Or you may be very wealthy in which case you can switch it On!

2 Make sure Cellular Data is **On**

You may want to use **Data Roaming** to get online if you are away from your home country. *Note*: Roaming charges for internet access are high so be careful if you switch this to On. In general, it is better to leave this switched OFF!

● You can view your account, review your data plan, **Add Data** or **Change Plan** (from pay-as-you-go to monthly), and Edit User Information

● **APN Settings** will vary depending on your carrier

● You can set up a **SIM PIN**

● Under **SIM Applications** you will see lots of services provided by your cellular carrier

# Set Up Your Wallpaper

Just like your Mac or PC, you can change the picture displayed at the Lock Screen and the background you see behind the apps. You can alter both of these using the in-built iPad wallpapers or you can use your own pictures.

Apple has already provided some excellent images but you may want more. There are several websites offering wallpapers and one of the best is **interfacelift.com** which offers stunning photos for Mac and PC – these work well on the iPad as well.

## Changing the wallpaper

**1** Go to **Settings > Wallpaper**

**2** Tap on the **Choose a New Wallpaper** option

There are 34 different Apple backgrounds that can be used as wallpaper. These include **Dynamic** backgrounds that appear to move independently from the apps icon layer above, and **Stills** backgrounds.

The **Display & Brightness** setting can be used to change the screen brightness and also change the font size, for apps that support this feature.

**3** Select **Apple Wallpaper** or **Photos**, to select a wallpaper from your own photo collection on the iPad

**4** Tap to make your choice and decide whether you want the new image as only wallpaper or Lock Screen, or both

# General Settings

### About

This provides full information about your iPad, Serial Number, number of apps installed, songs, and much more.

### Software Update

This can be used to check the version of iOS that you are using and install updates if they are available.

### Siri

Use this to set the language and voice style for the Siri voice assistant function.

### Spotlight Search

Determines the types of items that appear in the Spotlight Search window.

### Accessibility

Use this to set a variety of accessibility features for vision, hearing, learning and physical and motor conditions.

### Gestures

This setting allows you to pinch to activate the Home screen, swipe up (four fingers) to reveal the Multitasking bar (or also click twice on the Home button) or swipe left or right to move between running apps.

### Use Side Switch to:

You can configure the Side Switch to lock rotation, or activate the Mute function. (The Side Switch is not included on the iPad Air 2 but it is on all other models of iPad).

### Storage & iCloud Usage

This tells you how much space you have taken up on your iPad with apps and content and also your iCloud usage.

### Background App Refresh

This can be used to allow apps to be updated automatically when your iPad has online access through Wi-Fi or a cellular service.

Don't forget

There is a specific setting for **Sounds**, where you can configure the alert sounds for new mail arriving, sent mail, Calendar and social networking app alerts, lock sounds and keyboard clicks.

76

## Auto-Lock

This locks the screen if there is no input after a set period. You can select between 2-15 minutes or Never. Something around five minutes is probably the most practical. Once the Auto-Lock is activated you will need to re-enter your four-digit PIN at the Lock Screen to use the iPad.

## Restrictions

Useful if the iPad will be used by children. You can limit access to specific apps and also prohibit the installation of apps.

## Lock/Unlock

This can be used to automatically lock or unlock your iPad, through the use of an iPad cover.

## Date & Time

Choose the 12- or 24-hour clock. Set Time Zone, Date and Time.

## Keyboard

Here you can enable and disable Auto-Correction, Auto-Capitalization of the first letter in sentences, Enable Caps Lock and "." Shortcut (two taps on the spacebar to generate a period).

## Language & Region

This allows you to select keyboards in different languages.

## iTunes Wi-Fi Sync

This can be used to automatically sync the contents of your iPad with iTunes on your computer, when your iPad is connected to Wi-Fi. In iTunes on your computer you have to also check **Sync with this iPad over Wi-Fi** on.

## VPN

Lets you see your VPN (Virtual Private Network) connection if you use one, or the wireless network to which you are connected.

## Reset

Use this to reset all of your iPad settings, network settings, the keyboard, the Home screen layout and location and privacy settings.

## Profile

This is where security certificates can appear for specific apps or the iOS.

Hot tip

Some models of iPad (iPad Air 2 and later, and iPad Mini 3 and later) have a Touch ID sensor so that your iPad can only be unlocked by your own unique fingerprint. The setting **Touch ID & Passcode** can be used to set up the Touch ID for the Home button.

On other versions of the iPad, the **Passcode** settings can be used to create a 4- or 6-figure passcode for unlocking your iPad.

# Mail, Contacts, Calendars

This is the hub that lets you set up your email accounts, your contacts and your calendars.

## Mail

**1** Tap **Settings > Mail, Contacts, Calendars**

**2** Tap **Add Account...**

**3** Decide which type to use if you know this. You can choose from Microsoft Exchange, iCloud, Google Mail, Yahoo! Mail, or AOL. If you are uncertain, tap Other...

**4** Enter your full name, email address and password

**5** Give the account a **Description**, e.g. "Work Email"

**6** Click **Save** and Mail will configure the account for you

## Accounts

You can configure Mail to switch on Mail, Contacts, Calendars and Bookmarks for iCloud (cloud) syncing. You can also switch **Find My iPad** to On if you want to use this feature.

You will see the account information displayed under **Settings > Mail, Contacts, Calendars > Accounts**.

## Review the settings for the Mail app

**Preview** – how many lines of the email do you want to preview?

**Show To/Cc Label** – show or hide this option.

**Swipe Option** – tap on this for options for what appears when you swipe left or right on an email in your Inbox.

**Flag Style** – this determines the color and shape of flags that are used on emails.

**Ask Before Deleting** – switch to **On** as a safety measure, preventing the unwanted deletion of emails.

Hot tip

Find My iPad is free so set it up and use it if you lose your iPad.

**Load Remote Images** – if an email contains images and you want to see these, switch to **On**.

**Organize By Thread** – drag this **On** to view email conversations combined into individual threads.

**Always Bcc Myself** – for blind copies sent to yourself.

**Mark Addresses** – use this to add flags to certain types of email addresses.

**Increase Quote Level** – this indents messages that you forward to people.

**Signature** – assign a signature for the end of each email.

### Contacts

**Sort Order** – sort your contacts by first or last name.

**Display Order** – same as above.

**Short Name** – select the format for abbreviated names.

**My Info** – view your own details within the **Contacts** app.

**Contacts Found in Mail** – this can be turned **On** to enable auto-suggestions when entering contacts as email recipients.

### Calendars

**Time Zone Override** – switch to **Off** to display events for your current location.

**Alternate Calendars** – select calendars for different languages.

**Week Numbers** – Turn **On** to show week numbers for the current year, at the start of the week.

**Show Invitee Declines** – show any declined calendar invites.

**Sync** – set a timescale for syncing your calendar events.

**Default Alert Times** – set alert times for certain events.

**Start Week On** – set a day for your calendar to start on.

**Default Calendar** – select the default calendar for new events.

# Safari Settings

**Search Engine** – select Google, Yahoo!, Bing or DuckDuckGo.

**Search Engine Suggestions** – use this to display suggestions as you type into the Address bar or a search engine.

**Safari Suggestions** – use this to display suggestions as you type into the Spotlight search box.

**Quick Website Search** – turn this **On** to use the Smart Search Field for searching using a website name and then a specific keyword, to search for it on the selected website.

**Preload Top Hit** – use this to enable Safari to start loading the top result from a search, to make it quicker to access it.

**Passwords & AutoFill** – two options that can be used to remember your passwords and details entered into forms.

**Frequently Visited Sites** – this can be used to display your most visited sites, when you open a new tab or web page.

**Favorites** – use this for what is displayed on the Favorites page, when you open a new tab or enter an address in the Address bar.

**Open New Tabs in Background** – use this if you want to open new tabs while you are still viewing the current page.

**Show Favorites Bar** – use this to show or hide the Favorites bar (this is displayed at the top of the Safari window).

**Show Tab Bar** – use this to show all open tabs on the Tab Bar.

**Block Pop-ups** – leave **On** to avoid annoying pop-ups.

**Do Not Track** – turn this **On** if you do not want any details of your web browsing to be stored.

**Block Cookies** – many sites insist on allowing cookies but you can clear all the cookies (see Clear History and Website Data).

**Fraudulent Website Warning** – it is wise to be alerted when you visit potentially fraudulent sites so leave this **On**.

**Clear History and Website Data** – tap on this to delete details of your web browsing history and stored website data.

**Advanced** – a range of advanced settings, such as using JavaScript.

Hot tip

AutoFill is useful and saves you having to type your personal details into website forms.

# More Settings

## Maps

**Distances** – whether distances on maps are shown in kilometers or miles.

**Map Labels** – turn labels in English on or off.

## Music

**Show Apple Music** – turn this **On** to view the Apple Music option within the Music app. This is a subscription service that provides access to the full music catalogue in the iTunes Library.

**Sort Albums** – this determines the default of how content is displayed in the Music app.

**iCloud Music Library** – this can be used to access your music from different devices, via iCloud.

**iTunes Match** – any music on your iPad that is on iTunes is added to iCloud so you can listen to it on any device.

**Playback.** This has options for the **EQ** (equalizer) which enhances the audio output; **Volume Limit** to help prevent hearing damage by limiting the volume of playback; and **Sound Check**, that evens out the volume between different tracks.

## Videos

**Start Playing** – the default is sensibly set to **Where I Left Off** so you can stop watching a movie and resume later.

**Show iTunes Purchases** – display all purchased movies and TV shows within the app.

The **Notes** and **Reminders** apps also have their own Settings.

There is a range of **Privacy** settings where you can turn on **Location Services** so that specific apps can use your current geographic location.

The **Battery** settings can be used to display the remaining amount of battery power on the iPad's status bar and also how much battery usage each app is consuming.

**...cont'd**

### FaceTime

Enter the email address you want to use with FaceTime. If you don't want to be contacted using FaceTime you can switch it off.

### Photos & Camera

**Sharing options** – select options for sharing your photos to your own devices with iCloud and your Photo Stream (for more details, see Chapter Six, page 119).

**Photos Tab** – turn this on or off to show or hide summaries of your photos.

There are also settings for social networking sites, including Facebook and Twitter, which enable you to log in to these accounts and link them to iOS 9.

**Camera** – use this to turn a grid on or off for the camera, to help with composing photos.

**82**

**High Dynamic Range** – use this to blend the best exposures from three photos, while keeping the originals too.

### App and iTunes Stores

This is where you set up your account details for the App and iTunes Store.

Tap on the account name to see your details, including address, phone number and credit card.

**Automatic Downloads** – select which items out of Music, Apps, Books and Updates you want to be downloaded automatically, when you are connected to online services over Wi-Fi.

Setting up iTunes alerts is not obvious. To set up alerts go to **Settings >App and iTunes Stores** then tap **Apple ID**. Then tap **View Apple ID**. Sign in with your password and scroll down to **My Alerts**. Set up your alerts from the options shown.

# 4 Browsing the Web

*Browsing the web is probably the most popular activity on desktop and laptop computers so it comes as no surprise that the same is true of the iPad. Safari is pre-installed on the iPad and is a clean, fast browser that will more than satisfy all of your browsing needs.*

# Around Safari

The Safari app is the default web browser on the iPad.
This can be used to view web pages, save Favorites and read pages
with the Reader function. To start using Safari:

**1** Tap on the **Safari** app

**2** Tap on the Address Bar at the top of the Safari window.
Type a web page address

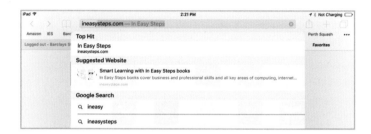

**3** Tap on the **Go** button on the keyboard
to open the web page, or select one
of the suggested options below the
Address Bar

**4** The selected
page opens
with the
top toolbar
visible. As you
scroll down
the page this
disappears

to give you a greater viewing area. Tap on the top of the
screen or scroll back up to display the toolbar again

# Navigating Pages

When you are viewing pages within Safari there are a number of functions that can be used:

**1** Tap on these buttons to move forward and back between web pages that have been visited

**2** Tap here to view Bookmarked pages, Reading List pages and Shared Links

**3** Tap here to add a bookmark, add to a Reading List, add an icon to your iPad Home screen, email a link to a page, share via social media or print a page

**4** Tap here to add a new tab

**5** Tap on a link on a page to open it. Tap and hold to access additional options, to open in a new tab, add to a Reading List or copy the link

**6** Tap and hold on an image and tap on **Save Image** or **Copy**

**Hot tip**

Tap and hold on the **Forward** and **Back** buttons to view lists of previously-visited pages in these directions.

**Hot tip**

The **Reading List** is similar to Bookmarks and you can use it to save pages that you want to read later. Also, you can read them when you are offline. The Reading List can be accessed from the button in Step 2.

# Opening New Tabs

Safari supports tabbed browsing, which means that you can open separate pages within the same window and access them by tapping on each tab at the top of the page:

**1** Tap here to open a new tab for another web page

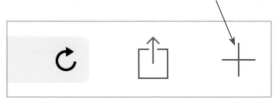

**2** Open a new page by entering a web address into the Address Bar, or tap on one of the thumbnails in the **Favorites** window

**3** Tap on the tab headings to move between tabbed pages

If there are too many items to be displayed on the Favorites Bar, tap on this button to view the other items.

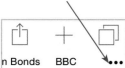

**4** Tap on the cross at the top of a tab to close it

# Tab View

This functionality gives you the ability to view all of your open Safari tabs on one screen. To use this:

**1** Tap here to activate Tab View

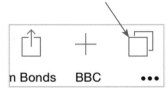

**2** All of the currently open tabs are displayed. Tap on one to open it

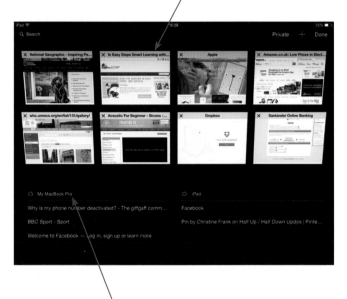

**3** If you have open Safari tabs on other Apple devices, these will be shown at the bottom of the window

**4** Tap on this button at the top of the window to open another tab

**5** Tap on this button to open a **Private** tab, where no browsing record will be recorded from this tab during the browsing session

**Hot tip**

Tab View can also be activated by pinching inwards with thumb and forefinger on a web page that is at normal magnification, i.e. 1 to 1.

**Don't forget**

Tap on the **Done** button at the top of the Tab View window to exit this and return to the web page that was being viewed when Tab View was activated.

# Bookmarking Pages

Once you start using Safari you will soon build up a collection of favorite pages that you visit regularly. To access these quickly they can be bookmarked, so that you can then go to them in one tap. To set up and use Bookmarks:

**1** Open a web page that you want to bookmark. Tap here to access the sharing options

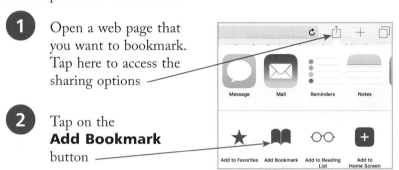

**2** Tap on the **Add Bookmark** button

**3** Tap on this link and select whether to include the bookmark on the Favorites Bar or in a Bookmarks folder

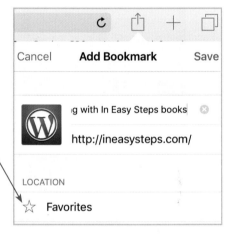

**4** Tap on the **Save** button

The Favorites Bar appears underneath the Address Bar in Safari. This includes items that have been added as Bookmarks.

**5** Tap here to view all of the bookmarks. The Bookmarks folders are listed. Tap on the **Edit** button at the bottom of the panel to delete or rename the folders

Edit

# Safari History

All of your web browsing will leave a history trail behind. This is useful if you want to revisit sites (*you should have saved a bookmark!*). Over time, the history list will become huge so it's a good idea to clear this from time to time. In addition, other people using your iPad can see your history and there may be sites you visit which you would prefer to keep private!

## Clear the history

**1** Go to **Settings > Safari**

**2** Tap **Clear History and Website Data**

**3** You will be asked to confirm this action

**4** Tap **Clear** and the history will be cleared

Beware

If you clear your history and website data, Safari will not remember any websites that you have visited or any other items from sites, so it will not be able to suggest website names when you start entering them into the address bar.

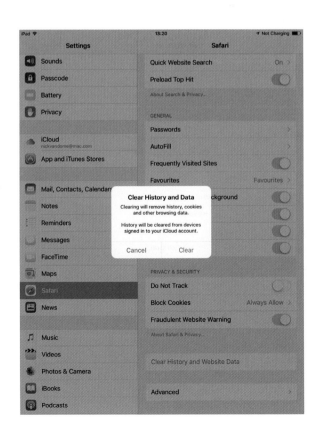

# Add Links to Home Screen

The various iPad screens are home to all of your apps, but you can also add web pages as buttons to the Home screen, to make finding and opening these easier. You wouldn't want all of your saved websites to be added to the Home screen or you would have very little room for actual apps. But for websites that are very important, or that you visit regularly, consider adding them to the Home screen.

**1** Navigate to a site you want to save

**2** Tap the **Share** icon

**3** Choose **Add to Home Screen**

You can also share web page links to the Notes app. This creates a note with a link to the required website.

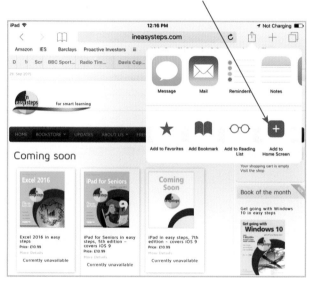

**4** Name the saved link and tap on the **Add** button

**5** The web page will resemble an app on the Home screen

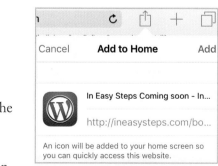

**6** Tap it and it will open Safari and take you straight to the correct web page

# Safari Privacy

We have already looked at the history and clearing this from time to time. The other item worth clearing on the iPad (and regular computer browsers, for that matter) is the Cookies file. This is a file containing sites you have visited, and the entries are made by the sites themselves. They don't necessarily do any major harm but for reasons of privacy it is a good idea to clear Cookies periodically.

**1** Go to **Settings > Safari** – Tap **Block Cookies**

For peace of mind, clear Cookies and History from time to time, as described on page 89.

**2** Select one of the options for blocking cookies

# Other Web Browsers

Safari is the default pre-installed browser on the iPad but there are others which include:

- Opera Mini (*shown below*)

- Atomic Web

- Privately

- Mercury Web Browser

- Safe Browser

- Browser plus

Some of these are written specifically for the iPad while others are for the iPhone but can be used on the iPad.

### What are the advantages of using third-party browsers?

- Many offer private browsing (no history retained)

- If you get bored with Safari and fancy a change try out one of these other ones and see if it suits your needs better

# 5 Mail and Text

*Love it or loathe it, email is a fact of life. We need to deal with email both at work and at home. Mail on the iPad makes reading and sending emails a pleasure, and in this chapter we will look at how to set up your accounts, manage your Inbox, and make the most of IMAP email.*

# What is Mail?

Some of us spend much of our time on PCs and Macs checking and sending emails. This is true also of mobile devices like the iPhone, BlackBerry and other handhelds. So, not surprisingly, a fair amount of your time on the iPad may be spent doing emails.

The Mail app built-in to the iPad is a feature-rich program that is easy to set up and use. It is similar to Mail, which comes with every Mac PowerBook and Mac desktop, although a few features are lacking. There's no stationery option on the iPad version and you can't have multiple signatures.

## Setting up an Email Account

**1** Go to **Settings > Mail, Contacts, Calendars** and tap on the **Add Account** link

**2** You will see a list of options

**3** Choose the one that matches your email account

**4** If you can't see it, select **Other** – enter your details including email address and password. The program will work out the rest for you

# POP or IMAP?

For most people these are fairly confusing terms but it's worth having a look at both types before setting your accounts up. POP stands for *Post Office Protocol* and IMAP means *Internet Message Access Protocol*. These are the two most common standards for email retrieval. POP3 is the current version of POP and is used for web-based email such as Google Mail. Rather than look at the nuts and bolts of these two systems we can summarize the pros and cons of each.

For Mail, IMAP email offers many advantages over POP3.

### IMAP lets you see all of your emails using any machine

If you use multiple computers – including handhelds such as BlackBerry or iPad – IMAP allows you to see your various mail folders from any device. The folder structure and the emails within the folders are the same because the folders and emails are kept on a central server (*not* on your computer or iPad).

| iPad 🔋 | | |
| --- | --- | --- |
| | **Mailboxes** | Edit |
| ✉ Inbox | | 4 > |
| ★ VIP | | ⓘ > |
| ● Flagged | | > |
| MAILBOXES | | |
| 🗋 Drafts | | 9 > |

When you set up a POP3 account you will see folders for Inbox, Sent Mail, Trash but no subfolders or the opportunity to create subfolders to categorize and file your emails. But with an IMAP account you can create as many folders and subfolders (and sub-subfolders) as you like and file all of your emails. You can browse all of your IMAP folders and emails on the iPad and transfer new emails into their respective folders, just as you would with paper mail using a file cabinet. There is a downside to IMAP though – since the emails are stored on a server which may be in the US (iCloud emails are currently stored in California), if you have no internet connection you may not be able to see your emails.

### So, which should you use?

If your email provider, e.g. Apple (iCloud), provides IMAP then select that. If POP3 is the only option you have, there's not much you can do to change this. For those of us wishing to archive emails and retrieve them months or years later, IMAP is the best possible solution.

# Composing an Email

**1** Open **Mail** by tapping its icon and decide which account you want to use (if you have more than one) by tapping **Accounts** and choosing one

**2** Tap the **New email** icon

**3** Enter the name of the recipient. As you start typing, Mail will present you with a list of possible options. Choose the recipient from the list if it is there

**4** Tap the **Subject** box and enter the email subject here

**5** Tap the main body of the email and type the text of your email

**Hot tip**

You can add signatures to your emails (Go to **Settings > Mail, Contacts, Calendars > Signature**). You can choose one generic signature or create a specific signature for each email account.

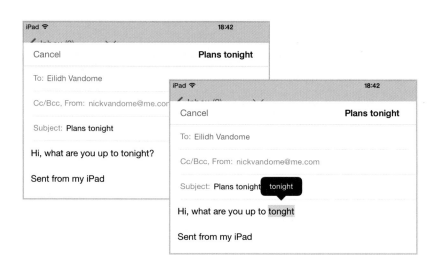

Type (or use Voice Dictation – see icon to the left of the keyboard if on Wi-Fi)

Mail will spot mistakes and suggest the correct word

**6** If you want to copy someone in on the email use the **Cc** box. To send a blind copy (the primary email recipient cannot see that a blind copy has been sent to another person, hence the term "blind"), tap the **Bcc** box

**7** Check the **spelling** – any errors will be underlined with a red dotted line. Correct by tapping on the misspelled word and choosing from available options, or delete the word and retype if Mail does not offer the correct word

**8** Once you're happy with the content and spelling, tap **Send** and your email will be sent

## Attach files to an email

At present you cannot attach files in the same way as you would with a regular computer – there's no real "desktop" or filing system you can see in order to find and attach a file. However, it can be done by pressing and holding within an email, see tip.

You can also send files such as documents and photos by sharing via email from *within* an app.

For example, in the Photos app there is an option to share photos by email. You can email Safari web pages from within the Safari app, and document management programs like Documents To Go allow you to email files from within the Documents To Go app.

You can add a photo or a video directly into an email by pressing and holding in the body of the email and tapping on the **Insert Photo or Video** button. You can then select the required item from the Photos app.

97

Here, a photo has been opened in Photos. To email the photo, tap the Share icon (top right) and select **Mail** from the dropdown menu options.

This option can be found in many apps on the iPad.

# Receiving and Reading Emails

Emails are "pushed" through to the iPad from the email server if your iPad is online. You can tell there are unread emails by looking for the badge on the app's icon.

## Manually checking for email

You can make Mail check for new email by pulling down on the email list.

## Reading emails in portrait mode

If you hold the iPad in portrait mode you will see a separate, floating account window, listing emails in the Inbox.

**1** Tap an email in the list and it will fill the whole screen

**2** To see the next or previous email tap the up or down arrows ∧ ∨ or tap Inbox again. Next to the word **Inbox** you may see (3) which means you have three unread emails in the Inbox

**3** When reading emails you can: **Move** the email 🗀 **Delete** 🗑, **Reply or Reply All** ↩, **Forward** the email to someone else ↩, **Compose** a new email ✐ and Flag an email ⚑

## Reading emails in landscape mode

**1** Tap the email you want to read – it will be displayed in the right-hand pane

**2** If you want to navigate to other folders in your account, tap the name of the account (top left) and you will see a folder list

**3** Scroll up or down until you find the folder you want, then tap it. You will then see the emails contained within that folder

Hot tip

Manual send and receive will save power. It is also the best way to retrieve email if you are using Data Roaming. To turn off Push, go to **Settings** > **Mail, Contacts, Calendars** > **Push** and drag the **Push** button to **Off**.

# ...cont'd

**4** Navigate back up the hierarchy by tapping the previous location link at the top

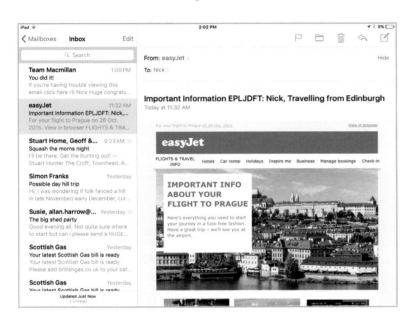

# Searching for Emails

Mail provides a simple Search box at the top left below the account name. You can search: **From**, **To**, **Subject**, **All**.

**Hot tip**

Searching for emails is usually quicker than looking for them manually.

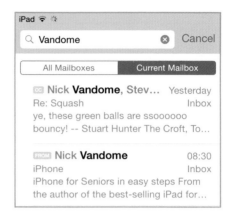

### Searching for emails across multiple accounts

You can also search for emails using the Spotlight search:

**1** Go to **Spotlight** search (press and hold on an empty space on a Home screen and swipe downwards)

**2** **Enter your search terms** into the search box

**3** Spotlight will then search all of your emails (and also Calendars, Contacts, Music, etc. unless you have configured Spotlight so it only searches emails)

**4** Once the email you are looking for is listed in the search list, tap it and Mail will open, and take you to that email open on the screen

# Deleting Unwanted Emails

We all receive email spam or emails we don't want to keep.
It's easy to delete emails, either singly or in batches.

### Delete a single email

**1** If the email you want to delete is open on the
screen, simply tap the **Trash** icon and the email
will be sent to the Trash folder

**2** If you are looking at a list of emails in the account
window, tap **Edit** then tap the radio button next to the
email you want to delete. Then hit **Trash**. The numbers
in brackets tell you that one email has been selected for
Delete or Move

**3** Another way of deleting emails is to view the list in the
accounts window then drag your finger across the email
from right to left and a **Trash** button will appear. Tap
this and the email will be deleted

Tap on the **More** button
in Step 3 to access more
options, including moving
the email to Junk. Tap
on the **Flag** button to
add a flag to the email,
to make it easier to find.

Deleted emails can
usually be salvaged from
the Trash if you want to
recover them. Within the
Trash folder, look down
the list for emails you
want to recover from the
Trash. Tap **Edit** and tap
the **radio button**
of the email you want
to recover. Tap **Move**
and choose **Inbox**. The
message will move from
Trash to Inbox.

# Adding Mailboxes

Different categories of email messages can be managed via Mailboxes. For instance, you may want to keep your social emails separately from ones that apply to financial activities.

**1** From your Inbox, tap on the **Mailboxes** button

**2** The current mailboxes are displayed. Tap on **Edit**

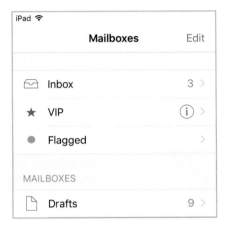

**3** Tap on **New Mailbox** at the bottom of the Mailboxes panel

**4** Enter a name for the new mailbox. Tap on the **Save** button

**5** Tap on the **Done** button

**6** To delete a mailbox, tap on it, then tap on the **Delete Mailbox** button

**Hot tip**

Messages can be edited within individual mailboxes. To do this, select a mailbox and tap once on the **Edit** button. The message can then be edited with the **Delete**, **Move** or **Mark** options at the bottom of the window.

**Don't forget**

Emails can be organized into specific folders. To do this, with the email open tap the **Folder** icon:

Decide which folder you want to use to store the email.

Tap on the folder name and the email will move across into its new location.

Move back to the main account level and tap on the folder name to view its contents.

# Messaging

Text messaging is now a commonly used method for keeping in touch. On your iPad you can join the world of text with the Apple iMessage service that is accessed via the Messages app. This enables text and media messages to be sent, free of charge, between users of the iOS (from version 5 onwards) operating systems, on the iPad, iPhone and iPod Touch. iMessages can be sent to cell/mobile phone numbers and email addresses. To use iMessages:

**1** Tap once on the **Messages** app

**2** You have to sign in with your Apple ID before you can use Messages. Enter these details and tap on the **Sign In** button

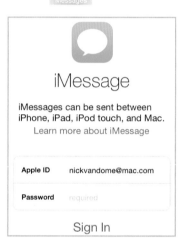

**iMessage**

iMessages can be sent between iPhone, iPad, iPod touch, and Mac.
Learn more about iMessage

| Apple ID | nickvandome@mac.com |
|---|---|
| Password | required |

Sign In

**Beware**

If a number, or an email address, is not recognized it shows up in red in the **To** box.

**3** Tap once on this button to create a new message and start a new conversation

**4** Tap once on this button to select a recipient from your contacts

**5** Tap once on a contact to select them as the recipient of the new message

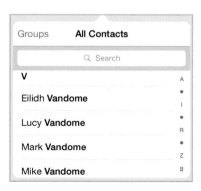

| Groups | **All Contacts** |
|---|---|

Q Search

**V**

Eilidh **Vandome**

Lucy **Vandome**

Mark **Vandome**

Mike **Vandome**

## ...cont'd

### Creating iMessages

To create and edit messages and conversations:

**1** Tap once here and type with the keyboard to create a message. Tap once on the **Send** button

**2** As the conversation progresses each message is displayed here

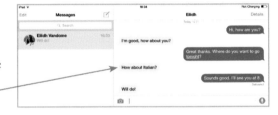

**3** To edit whole conversations, tap once on the **Edit** button in the Messages panel

Edit

**4** Tap once here and tap once on the **Delete** button to delete the conversation

Delete

### Sending Photos and Videos

Within Messages in iOS 9 it is possible to add different types of media to a text message, including photos and videos. To do this:

**1** To add a photo or a video, tap once on the camera icon next to the text field. Select an item from your **Photo Library** or take a photo or video

**2** The Camera apps opens. Select the photo or video option and capture by tapping on the shutter button

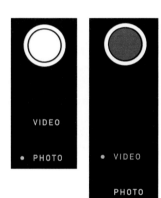

If you do not like a photo or video that you have taken, tap once on the **Retake** button and try again.

Retake

**3** Tap once on the **Use Photo** or **Use Video** button

Use Photo

Use Video

**4** The photo or video is added to the text field, where new text can also be added

...cont'd

### Adding Audio Clips

You can also send family and friends audio messages in an iMessage so that they can hear from you too. To do this:

**1** Press and hold on the microphone icon at the right-hand side of the text field

**2** Create your audio clip and tap once here to send it

**3** Tap once here to delete the current clip and start recording again

### Sending your location

With Messages, you can now also show people your location (by sending a map) rather than just telling them. To do this:

**1** Once a conversation has started, tap once on the **Details** button

Details

**2** Tap once on the **Send My Current Location**, or **Share My Location** buttons

| LOCATION |
| --- |
| Send My Current Location |
| Share My Location |

**3** For Share My Location, tap once on one of the options for how long you want your location to be shared for

| Share for One Hour |
| --- |
| Share Until End of Day |
| Share Indefinitely |

**Hot tip**

If you select **Share My Location**, this will be updated if your location changes (as long as Location Services are turned On, **Settings > Privacy > Location Services**).

# 6 Photos

*The iPad app, Photos, delivers rich-looking photos at high resolution so you can view all of your albums as slideshows, or share them with family and friends.*

# Getting Photos onto the iPad

Because of its high resolution display and rich colors, the iPad is perfect for viewing photos. The iPad supports pictures in a number of formats including JPEG, TIFF, GIF and PNG. But how do you get your photos onto the iPad in the first place, in addition to using either of the two iPad cameras?

### Importing from a computer program

**1** You can import from Aperture on the Mac or from Adobe Photoshop Album 2.0 or later, or Adobe Photoshop Elements 3.0 or later

**2** Use iTunes to configure which albums you want to sync and also remove from selected albums

### Using the Lightning to SD Card Camera Reader

**1** Plug in the Lightning to SD Card Camera Reader

**2** **Insert the SD card** from your camera

**3** Click **Import Photos**

**4** You will be asked whether you want to keep or delete the photos on the SD card

**5** View your photos by tapping the **Photos** app

### Using the Lightning to USB Camera Adapter

**1** Plug the Lightning to USB Camera Adapter into the iPad

**2** **Attach the camera** using the camera cable

**3** Make sure the camera is turned **On** and is in transfer mode

**4** Select the photos you want to import

The camera on the back of the iPad is an iSight one and is capable of capturing high resolution photos and also high definition videos. On the iPad Air 2, iPad Pro and iPad Mini 4 it is an 8 megapixel camera, on other models it is a 5 megapixel one. The front-facing one, a FaceTime camera, is better for video calls.

When importing photos from a camera you can also choose whether to keep the photos on the camera once they have been imported, or delete them.

# Adding Photos from Email

You can email a photo to yourself to open and download to your iPad, or add any photos you have received in an email in the same way.

**1** Open the email containing the photo or image

**2** Make sure you can see the image you want to import then tap and hold your finger on the image until you see a pop-up including **Message**, **Mail**, **Notes**, **Twitter**, **Facebook**, **Flickr**, **iCloud Photo Sharing**, **Quick Look**, **Save Image**, **Save Attachment**, **Markup and Reply**, **Assign to Contact**, **Copy** and **Print**

**3** Tap **Save Attachment** and the image will be sent to the **Photos** app on the iPad

Tap on the **Notes** option in Step 2 to create a new item in the **Notes** app, with the photo inserted.

## Saving photos or images from Safari web pages

**1** Tap and hold your finger on the image you want to save

**2** Hold your finger on the image until you see a pop-up saying **Save Image/Copy**

**3** The image will be sent to the **Photos** app on the iPad

# Viewing Photos

Once photos have been captured, they can be viewed and organized in the Photos app. To do this:

**1** Tap on the **Photos** app

**2** At the top level, all photos are displayed according to the years in which they were taken

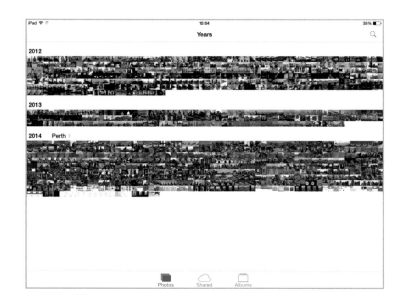

**3** Tap within the **Years** window to view photos according to specific, more defined, timescales. This is the **Collections** level

**Hot tip**

If you have iCloud set up, all of your photos will also be saved under the **All Photos** album in the **Albums** section. This enables all of your photos to be made available on any other devices you have with iCloud, such as an iPhone, an iPod Touch or a Mac computer.

**Don't forget**

Tap on the **Photos**, **Shared** and **Albums** buttons at the bottom of the **Years**, **Collections** or **Moments** windows, to view the photos in each of these sections.

**4** Tap within the Collections window to drill down further into the photos, within the **Moments** window

For each section, tap on the previous location link in the top left-hand corner to move back up to the previous level.

**5** Tap on a photo within the **Moments** window to view it at full size

Double-tap with one finger on an individual photo to zoom in on it. Double-tap with one finger again to zoom back out. To zoom in to a greater degree, swipe outwards with thumb and forefinger.

**6** Swipe with one finger or drag here to move through all of the available photos in a specific Moment

# Creating Albums

Within the Photos app it is possible to create different albums in which you can store photos. This can be a good way to organize them according to different categories and headings. To do this:

**1** Tap on the **Albums** button

**2** Tap on this button

**3** Enter a name for the new album

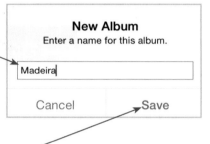

**New Album**
Enter a name for this album.

Madeira

Cancel          Save

**4** Tap on the **Save** button

**5** Tap on the photos you want to include in the album

Moments          Done

Add 7 photos to "Madeira".

Select

**6** Tap on the **Done** button

Done

**7** The new album is added to the Albums section in the Photos app

Madeira

# Selecting Photos

It is easy to take hundreds, or thousands, of digital photos and most of the time you will only want to use a selection of them. Within the Photos app it is possible to select individual photos so that you can share them, delete them or add them to albums.

**1** Access the Moments section and tap on the **Select** button

Press and hold on a photo to access an option to copy it, rather than selecting it.

**2** Tap on the photos you want to select, or tap on the **Select** button again to select all of the photos

To add items to an album, tap on this button in the **Moments** section.

**3** Tap on the **Deselect** button if you want to remove the selection

Tap on photos to select them, then tap on the **Add To** button and select either an existing album or tap on the **New Album** link to create a new album with the selected photos added to it.

**4** Use these buttons to, from left to right, share the selected photos, delete them or add them to an album

# Photos Slideshow

All, or some of your photos in the Photos app can be viewed in a continuous slideshow, and you can even add your own music to it. To do this:

**1** Tap an **Album** to open it

**2** Tap the **Slideshow** button (if you can't see the controls, tap the screen)

**3** Tap on the **Options** button on the bottom toolbar. Tap on the **Music** button to select a song from the music library (or select to have None)

**4** Tap on the **Theme** button to select an effect for when photos move from one to another. If you are showing the photos by connecting the iPad to a TV or AV projector use the Dissolve transition

**5** Tap **On** the **Repeat** option to play the slideshow more than once

**6** Tap on the **Play** button to play the slideshow, or the **Pause** button to pause it

**Hot tip**

Slideshows can also be created from specifically selected photos. Select the photos as shown on the previous page, tap on the **Share** button and tap on the **Slideshow** option from the menu.

# Emailing Your Photos

You can email your photos to family, friends or work colleagues, directly from the Photos app. To do this:

**1** Open the **Photos** app and locate the photo you wish to email using the relevant button at the bottom of the Photos app window

**2** Open a photo at full size, or tap on **Select** and tap on a photo to select it

**3** Tap the **Share** icon and choose **Mail**

**4** Mail will open with the photo already added to the message

**Hot tip**

If you are emailing very large photos (in terms of file size) check with the recipient first to ensure that their email client can accept large files.

**5** Compose the email and tap **Send**

...cont'd

## Copying and pasting a photo into an email

**1** Press and hold on a photo or image in **Photos**, on a web page or document

**2** Tap **Copy**

**3** Open **Mail** and select **New Message**

**4** Press and hold inside the email body

**5** Select **Paste** to paste the image into the email

## Emailing multiple photos

**1** Open a photo Album

**2** Tap **Select**

**3** Select photos to email (up to five at a time)

**4** Tap **Share** (top left) and choose **Mail**

**5** The photos will be inserted into a blank email

**Hot tip**

You can paste photos into an email. You can even paste multiple photos into the same email.

**Hot tip**

iOS 9 makes it incredibly easy to share your pictures with Facebook, Twitter, etc. Tap the **Share** icon and choose the relevant social network. If you have not added an account you'll be prompted to do so.

**Beware**

You can only share five pictures at a time using Mail. If you select more than five you will not see the Mail share option.

# Adding Photos to Contacts

It's easy and more personal to assign a photograph to your contacts than leaving them blank.

**1** Open **Contacts**

**2** Find the contact to which you want to add a photo

**3** Tap **Edit** next to the person's name

**4** Tap **Choose Photo**

**5** You will be presented with your photo albums and imported photos

**6** Select the photo you want to use

**7** Move and scale until you're happy with the size and position

**8** Tap **Use**

## Alternative method

**1** **Find a photo** and open it by tapping it

**2** Tap the **Share** icon

**3** Choose **Assign to Contact**

**4** Choose the contact you want, and voilà – the photo will be placed into the photo box for your contact

Personalize your contacts by adding photographs.

# Taking Photos and Videos

Because of its mobility and the quality of the screen, the iPad is excellent for taking and displaying photos. Photos can be captured directly using one of the two built-in cameras (one on the front and one on the back) and then viewed, edited and shared using the Photos app. To do this:

**1** Tap on the **Camera** app

**2** Tap on this button to capture a photo (or press the volume button at the side of the iPad)

**3** Tap on this button to swap between the front or back cameras on the iPad

The iPad cameras can be used for different formats:

**1** Swipe up or down at the side of the camera screen, underneath the shutter button, to access the different shooting options. Tap on the **Photo** button to capture photos at full-screen size

**2** Tap on the **Square** button to capture photos at this ratio

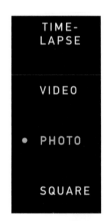

**3** Tap on the **Time-lapse** button and press the shutter button (which appears red with a ring around it) to create a time-lapse image: the camera keeps taking photos periodically until you press the shutter button again

**4** Tap on the **Video** button and press the red shutter button to take a video

# Camera Settings

## iCloud Sharing

Certain camera options can be applied within Settings. Several of these are to do with storing and sharing your photos via iCloud. To access these:

**1** Tap on the **Settings** app

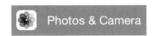

**2** Tap on the **Photos & Camera** tab

**3** Drag the **iCloud Photo Library** button to **On** to

upload your whole iPad photo library to the iCloud (it remains on your iPad too). Similarly, photos on your other Apple devices can also be uploaded to the iCloud and these will then be available on your iPad as well

**4** Select an option for storing iCloud

| Optimize iPad Storage | ✓ |
| Download and Keep Originals | |

photos. **Optimize iPad Storage** uses less storage as it uses device-optimized versions of your images, e.g. smaller file sizes

**5** Drag the **Upload to My Photo Stream** button to **On** to enable all new photos and

videos that you take on your iPad to be uploaded automatically to the iCloud

**6** Drag the **iCloud Photo Sharing** button to **On** to

allow you to create albums within the Photos app that can then be shared with other people via iCloud

*Don't forget*

If the **iCloud Photo Library** option is **On** then your photos will all appear in the **All Photos** album in the Albums section, as well as in the Photos section. If iCloud Photo Library is **Off** there will be a **Camera Roll** album in the Albums section, where photos created on your iPad will appear.

*Don't forget*

Drag the **Grid** button to On to place a grid over the screen when you are taking photos with the Camera, if required. This can be used to help compose photos by placing subjects using the grid.

# Use Photos as Wallpaper

Wallpaper, as well as being something you paste onto the walls of your house, is also the term for the backdrop used for the iPad screens. Apple has produced some gorgeous wallpapers for you to use but you can use your own images if you prefer.

**1** Find the photo you want to use in **Photos**

**2** Tap to open the picture at full size

**3** Tap the **Share** icon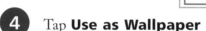

**4** Tap **Use as Wallpaper**

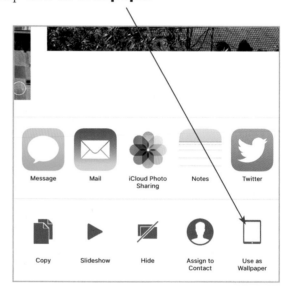

**Hot tip**

You can use your own photos as wallpapers, as well as images saved from the web and email.

**5** You will then have the option to use this for the **Lock Screen** or **Home Screen**, or both

# 7 Videos

*The iPad, with its Retina Display, is ideal for video. The high resolution screen and ease of use make Videos a perfect app for watching movies you have purchased through iTunes or converted from your own DVDs. You can also record video using the iPad's built-in cameras.*

# Getting Video onto the iPad

The iPad is a great multimedia device for watching movies, TV shows, video podcasts and other video content. The resolution of the screen makes movies crisp and clear. On the iPad, movies can be downloaded and viewed by using the **Videos** app.

### Different ways to get videos onto the iPad

- Buy or rent videos using iTunes on the iPad or computer

- Sync videos from the Mac or PC using iTunes

- Use email if the video is short

- Use the Photos app on the Mac

- From a folder on your hard drive

### Getting your own DVDs onto the iPad

You may have purchased (physical) DVDs and would like to watch them on your iPad. But how can you get them on there? There are several programs for both PC and Mac that will convert DVDs into a variety of formats for iPhone, Apple TV and iPad, such as MPEG-4, .M4V, .MOV, .MP4. Handbrake (**http://handbrake.fr**) is a free app available for both Mac and Windows platforms that makes the conversion easy.

Hot tip

Use Handbrake to convert your own DVDs into an appropriate format for the iPad.

Don't forget

Apple TV is a small box that can be connected to your TV or Apple devices to stream movies, music, TV programs and other media content from iTunes, YouTube, Netflix, etc. using Wi-Fi.

Handbrake has an iPad option at present but I use *AppleTV* which looks great on the iPad and Apple TV.

# Playing Videos

To play videos on the iPad you need to open the **Videos** app.

**1** Tap **Videos** to open the app. Click on the **Store** button

**2** Tap the **Category** you want to watch, e.g. **Movies**

**3** **Select** the title of the one you want

If the video has chapters you can choose a specific chapter to watch.

### Where are the controls?

You can use the scrubber bar to move forwards and backwards to a specific place in the video.

**1** Tap the **iPad screen** while the movie is playing

**2** The controls (**scrubber bar** and **volume**) will appear on screen

**3** Slide the **playhead** (filled circle) to where you want to view

You can't view your own videos in the Videos app – you can only view those in the Photos app.

The scrubber bar is the bar at the top of the video window that enables you to move through the content on the screen by dragging the playhead (see Step 3).

## ...cont'd

The video controls are fairly standard, and are similar throughout iPad apps that play video, including YouTube. The main ones to note in Videos are those that make the screen fill or fit the page. As well as tapping the icons, you can make the video fill the screen by double-tapping the screen while the movie is playing. Double-tapping again will make the video fit (not fill) the screen.

**Hot tip**

Tap the screen twice when a movie is playing to make it fill the screen. Tap twice again to make it fit the screen.

| | | |
|---|---|---|
| **Pause video** | Tap here to pause | ❚❚ |
| **Resume playing** | Tap here or press center button on Apple headset | ▶ |
| **Increase/decrease volume** | Drag volume slider control or use buttons on Apple headset | |
| **Start video over** | Tap and drag the playhead all the way to the LEFT or tap here | ⏮ |
| **Skip to next chapter (if video contains chapters)** | Tap here or press the center button twice on Apple headset | ⏭ |
| **Skip to previous chapter** | Tap here or press the center button three times on Apple headset | ⏮ |
| **Start playback at specific chapter** | Tap Chapter icon then select the chapter you want to view | |
| **Fast forward/Rewind** | Touch and hold these buttons | ⏭ ⏮ |
| **Move to specific point in video** | Drag playhead to desired point | |
| **Stop watching movie before the end** | Tap **Done** or the Home button to quit the Videos app | |
| **Scale video to fill screen** | Tap here to fill screen | ⤢ |
| **Scale video to fit screen** | Tap here to fit the screen | ⤡ |

# Purchased or Rented Movies

You can rent or buy movies from the iTunes Store. Also, if you have purchased movies using Apple TV, then these can also be synced to your iPad.

**1** Rent or buy movies from the iTunes Store. Allow the movie to download completely (you cannot watch the movie until it has fully downloaded)

**2** Tap the **Videos** app

**3** Tap **Movies**

**4** Tap the movie you want to watch

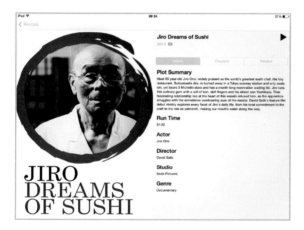

## Sync movies purchased on Mac, PC or Apple TV

**1** Connect the iPad to a computer

**2** Go to **iPad > Movies** pane in iTunes and check the movie(s) you want to sync to the iPad

**3** Click **Apply** then **Sync Now**

Beware

Movies rented on the iPad cannot be transferred to your computer.

Hot tip

Some music CDs have music videos included, or you may buy Music videos using Apple TV or from another source. These should show up in a separate section of Movies (Music Videos).

# Removing Videos from the iPad

To remove movies from your iPad:

## Remove a movie from the Videos app

**1** Tap **Videos** on the iPad Home Screen to open the app

**2** Tap and hold the movie you want to remove

**3** The **Delete** button will appear

**4** Tap the **X** icon to delete the movie

## Remove a movie using iTunes

**1** With the iPad connected to your computer

**2** Go to **iTunes > Movies**

**3** **Deselect** the movie you want to remove from the iPad

**4** Click **Apply** then **Sync**

The selected movie will be removed from the iPad. The movie will still remain on your computer, and if you want to sync it back to the iPad, check its radio button in iTunes.

**Hot tip**

If you delete a movie on the iPad you will still have a copy on your computer which you can use to resync the movie back to your iPad.

# Watch Movies on TV or Screen

You can connect your iPad to a TV or AV projector. You will need to buy an Apple Lightning to VGA Adapter or a Lightning Digital AV Adapter (for HDMI).

Apple Lightning to VGA Adapter

If you have Apple TV 2 or later you can wirelessly share your videos using AirPlay.

Apple Lightning Digital AV Adapter (allows HDMI output and charging of the iPad at the same time)

**1** **Connect the iPad** to the TV

**2** **Select PC** option using your TV's input controls

**3** Tap **Videos** to open the app, then select the movie you want to watch

You cannot play DRM movies on the TV or a screen using the VGA Connector.

### Not all movies can be played

Some movies will not play through the TV – those with DRM (Digital Rights Management) may not play and you may see a warning that you are not authorized to play the movie. The solution (though expensive) may be to buy the movie on physical DVD then run it through Handbrake (see page 122) using the Universal Option, and this should play fine through the TV.

# Recording and Editing Video

Recording videos using the iPad is as easy as taking still pictures. Once recorded, you can edit your video and trim unwanted footage, email or send your video to iCloud or YouTube, or share your video by sending to Apple TV.

**1** Tap on the **Camera** app

**2** Swipe up or down so that the **Video** button is highlighted

**3** Tap on this button to swap cameras from front to back, and vice versa

**4** Tap on this button to record a video. Tap on it again to stop recording

**5** Once the video has been captured it is saved within the **Photos** app with the video camera icon and the duration of the video showing on the thumbnail

**Don't forget**

The iSight camera on the iPad Air 2 can also capture slow-motion video, with the Slo-Mo option.

6 Click the thumbnail, then tap on this button in the middle of the screen to play the video

7 Tap on this button to share the video through the standard iPad options and also social networking sites, such as YouTube and Facebook (if you have accounts with these services)

**Hot tip**

To share your video on Facebook, go to your Facebook page via the Facebook app or the Facebook site (**www. facebook.com**) and follow instructions to upload videos.

...cont'd

### Editing videos

You cannot edit videos with the Photos app but there is a range of apps in the App Store that can be downloaded and used to edit your own videos.

### iMovie

This is the iPad version of the Apple video editing app and offers a wide range of editing options and effects.

### Finding apps

Access the App Store and enter **video editing** into the Search box to find a wider range of this type of app.

# 8 Keeping up with Events

*With your iPad in hand, you can always keep up-to-date with the latest news and events. The News app can be used to view news stories from a variety of selected sources and with the Podcast app you can listen to a range of audio and video broadcasts, covering topics from current affairs to comedy.*

After tapping on the **Get Started** button in Step 2 you will be asked if you want email alerts for the news feeds that you select. Tap on **Sign Me Up** or **Not Now**, as required.

Get News in Your Inbox

The best stories, selected just for you

Sign Me Up

Not Now

At the time of printing, the News app is only available in the US, the UK and Australia. It is gradually being rolled out to other regions.

# Getting the News

The News app replaces Newsstand, which was available in earlier versions of iOS. It is a news aggregation app that collates news stories from a variety of publications, covering a range of categories. To use the News app:

**1** Tap on the **News** app

**2** Tap on the **Get Started** button

Welcome to **News**

The best stories from the sources you love, selected just for you. The more you read, the more personalized your News becomes.

News and Privacy

Get Started

**3** Tap on news publications in which you are interested

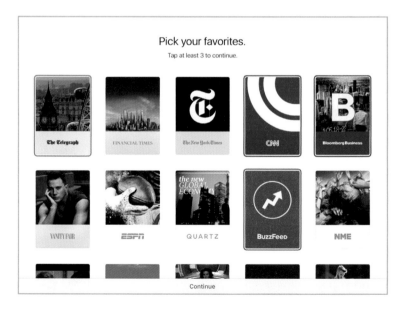

Pick your favorites.

Tap at least 3 to continue.

Continue

**4** Tap on the **Continue** button

Continue

**5** Items from the selected publications are displayed on the **For You** page

**6** News stories are presented in either video or text format

**Hot tip**

Tap on the **Search** button on the bottom toolbar to look for specific publications or subjects. These can then be added to your News feed and will appear under the **For You** and **Favorites** sections.

**7** Tap on the **Favorites** button on the bottom toolbar to view the publications that were added in Step 3

**...cont'd**

8 Tap on the **Edit** button to remove existing Favorite publications

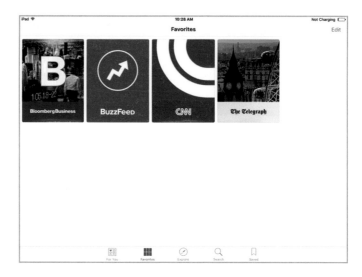

9 Tap on the **Explore** button to add more items

10 Select more publications or specific topics. These will be available on the **For You** page

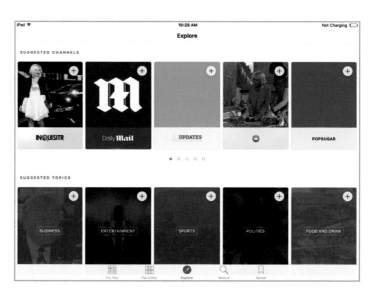

# Finding Podcasts

Podcasts are audio or video broadcasts that can be created by individuals or taken from programs that have been broadcast, usually on the radio. In iOS 9, the Podcasts app is one of the pre-installed ones and can be used to download podcasts. You can search for podcasts from within the Podcasts app:

1. Tap on the **Featured** button on the bottom toolbar to view the currently promoted podcasts

2. Swipe up and down the screen to view the range of Featured podcasts

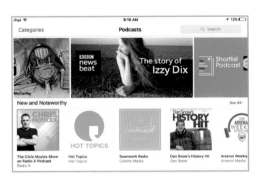

3. Tap on the **Top Charts** button to view the top ranking podcasts

4. Tap on a podcast to view its details

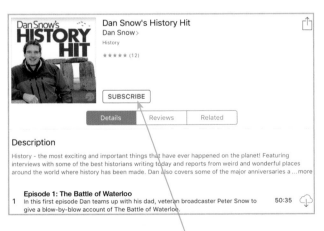

5. Tap on the **Subscribe** button to subscribe to the podcast and download this episode and subsequent ones

Tap on the **Categories** button in the Top Charts section to search for podcasts according to specific topics, such as Comedy, News & Politics, Music or Sports & Hobbies.

Categories

# Playing Podcasts

Podcasts to which you have subscribed can be played from within the Podcasts app:

**1** Tap on the Podcasts app and tap on the **My Podcasts** button to view podcasts to which you have subscribed

**2** Tap on a podcast to start playing it

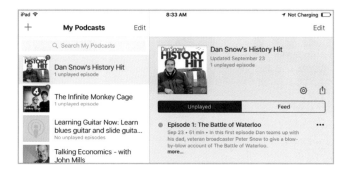

**3** Use these buttons on the bottom toolbar to move through the podcast in 15 minute intervals or pause and play it

**4** Tap on the **Unplayed** button to view podcasts that have been downloaded but not played

**5** Podcasts can either be in video or audio format

# 9 Calendar

*You can never be too organized!*
Calendar *makes it easy to set up*
*all of your appointments and also*
*store and share them using* iCloud.

# Calendar Navigation

The Calendar app has a clear layout and interface, making it easy to enter and edit appointments. The app is designed to resemble a physical calendar, with a left and right page. Each shows different items depending on which view you are using.

In the **Day** view, the left column shows that day's appointments, with any scheduled events spread out on the right. The **Week** view shows the whole seven days with all appointments clearly labeled. The **Month** view shows the whole month's appointments, and the **List** view shows both right and left pages with the current day on the right and the list of all appointments (the total Calendar appointments) in the left column. The example below is Day view.

**Hot tip**

You don't need to open the app to see the date – it shows on the app's icon even if it hasn't been opened, just like Calendar on the Mac.

View by Day, Week, Month or Year          Search   Add Event

Tap to go to Today    View available Calendars    View Invitations

# The Calendar Views

You can look at your Calendar using **Day**, **Week**, **Month**, or **Year** views.

Week view showing detailed information for each day

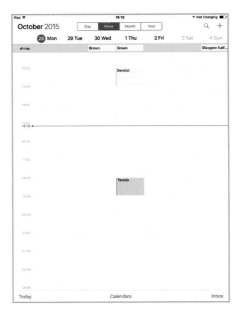

Month view

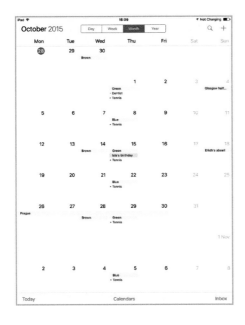

In Month view, you can scroll continuously through the calendar. This means that you do not have to just view a single month on its own, you can view the end of one month and the beginning of the next month in the same calendar window.

# Adding Events

You can add events (e.g. appointments) to Calendar directly on the iPad. If the calendar is turned on for iCloud, everything within the app will be available via iCloud and any compatible iCloud devices which also have the Calendar app.

## To add appointments directly onto the iPad

**1** Open the **Calendar** app

**2** Tap **+** at the top right of the Calendar window or press and hold on a specific date

**3** Enter a title for the event in the **Title** field

It's generally easier to add events using the Calendar app on a Mac computer especially if you have lots of events to add.

140

**4** Enter a location if necessary in the **Location** field

**5** Drag the **All-day** button to **Off**. Tap **Starts** and rotate dials to the required start time

**6** Tap **Ends** (One hour is the default since most meetings last an hour) to add the end time for the event. Rotate the dials in the same way as for the start time

**7** Tap **Repeat** if you want to repeat the event, e.g. anniversary, birthday

**8** If you want a reminder tap **Alert** (see image in Step 3)

**9** Tap **Calendar** to assign the event to a specific calendar if you have more than one (see image in Step 3)

Don't forget

Alerts can be added for different time periods, and the selection varies depending on how far in the future the event is scheduled for.

# Editing Calendar Events

This is very straightforward. Again, you can edit directly on the iPad using any of the views (Day, Week, Month or List). Tapping the appointment once in Day or List view takes you straight into edit mode.

**1** Tap the **event** to open it

**2** Tap **Edit**

**3** Amend the event, making your changes

**4** Tap **Done**

**Hot tip**

All elements of a calendar event can be edited, including changing it to an All-day event or changing the title and location.

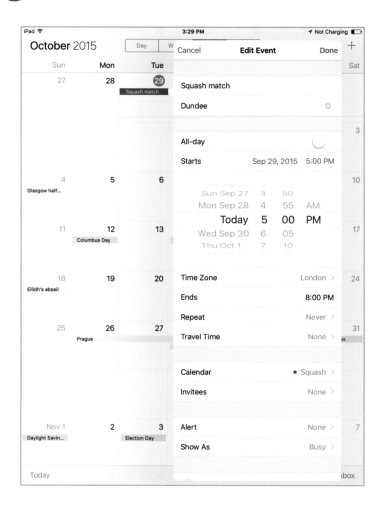

# Deleting Events

You can delete appointments using your computer or using the iPad. Either way, it's pretty simple.

**1** Tap **Calendar** and open the event by tapping it once. Tap on **Delete Event**, or

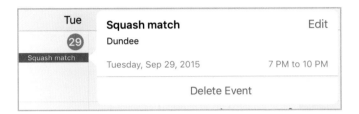

**2** Tap on **Edit** in the window above

**3** At the bottom of the window you will see **Delete Event**

If the Calendar is turned On for iCloud, any items that are deleted will also be deleted from any other of your iCloud-enabled Apple devices.

**4** Tap **Delete Event** to delete the event

# Calendar Alarms

How can you be sure you don't miss a crucial appointment? You could look at the Calendar app daily, or more often, and scan through all of the upcoming events.

But an easier way is to set an alarm, or a reminder if the event is really important. For example, you might want a reminder two days before an assignment has to be handed in.

On the iPad Calendar, reminders appear as notifications (with sound) on the screen. Set these up by going to **Edit** mode then tap **Alert**. Decide how far ahead you want the alert.

The alert shows as a notification on the screen (locked or unlocked), at the allocated time, and there will be an alarm sound so you cannot ignore the alert.

# 10 Contacts

*Gone are the days when we just stored contacts on a cell phone SIM card. The world of contacts has become much more advanced and Contacts makes it easy to add and view contacts, making all their details instantly available on your iPad.*

# Exploring the Contacts App

The Contacts app is a simple but elegant app for managing all of your contact information. The app is designed to resemble a physical address book, showing your **Contacts** and **Groups** down the left hand page with the selected contact's details shown on the right facing page.

Groups button      Search box      Add a new contact      Edit contact

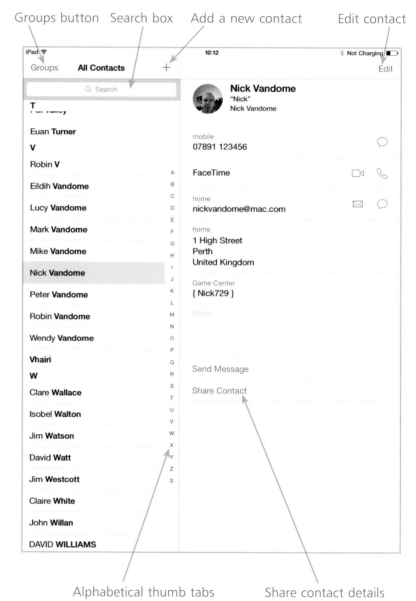

146

**Don't forget**

The Contacts app is another one which can be set up for iCloud, so that your contacts are stored here and are available from the online iCloud website, and any other iCloud-enabled Apple devices you have.

Alphabetical thumb tabs      Share contact details

You can also browse Contacts in landscape view but the details are much the same as portrait, although the pages are a bit wider.

Tap on a contact in the left-hand panel to view their details in the right-hand panel.

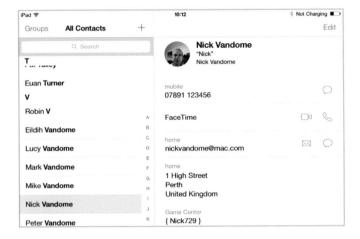

## Toggle between Groups and All Contacts

If you have groups, you can access these from within Contacts. Although you can add to a group, you cannot set up a group in Contacts – the group itself needs to be created using your computer Contacts app. To view your groups:

**1** Tap the **Groups** button to view all groups

**2** Tap a group name to select it and tap on the **Done** button to view the members in the group

**Beware**

You cannot create new groups in the Contacts app; you can only add to existing ones.

# Adding Contacts

You can add contacts directly onto the iPad.

To add a new contact:

**1** Launch **Contacts**

**2** Tap the **+** icon at the top of the left-hand page

**3** Enter details into the New Contact page, adding a photo if you wish

**4** Click **Done** when finished

**Hot tip**

Tap on the green **+** button next to a field to access additional options for it.

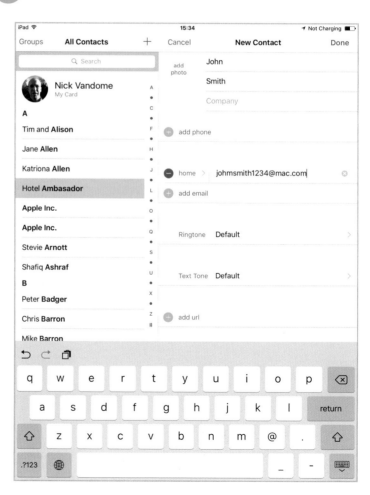

# Adding to Groups

With the Contacts app you can also view groups of people for areas such as hobbies, family or work. To do this:

**1** Launch Contacts and tap the **Groups** button to view all groups

**2** Tap a group name to select it

**3** Tap **Done** to view the contents of the group

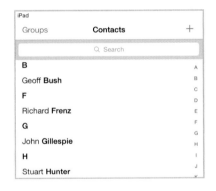

**4** Tap the **+** button to create a new entry for the group

**5** Enter the details for the new entry (the entry will be added to the group and also All Contacts in the Contacts app)

**6** Tap **Done**

**7** Tap the **Groups** button and tap on **All Contacts** to view everyone in your contacts. Tap **Done** to view your contacts

Beware

On the iPad, Groups in the Contacts app can be used to send a group email to the members of the group.

# Edit and Delete Contacts

### Edit a contact

This can be done directly on the iPad.

**1** Open the **Contacts** app

**2** Select the contact and tap on **Edit**

**3** Amend the details

**4** Tap **Done** when finished

**Hot tip**

Individual entries for a contact can be deleted by tapping on the red "–" symbol next to them and tapping on the **Delete** button.

### Delete a contact

You can delete contacts straight from your iPad. If you have iCloud set up for Contacts, then the contact will be deleted from all iCloud-enabled devices.

**1** Open the **Contacts** app

**2** Select the contact you want to delete

**3** Tap **Edit**

**4** Scroll to the bottom of the contact page

**5** Tap **Delete Contact**

# Assigning Photos

You won't want to have photos for all your contacts, but for family and friends it is great to have their picture displayed in the contacts list.

**1** Open **Contacts**

**2** Find the contact to which you want to assign a photo

**3** Tap **Edit** and tap on **add photo** next to their name

**4** Tap **Choose Photo**

**5** Select a photo from those stored on your iPad

**6** Tap **Use** or **Choose** when you are happy with your choice of photo

Add photos to friends and family contacts – it makes it more personal.

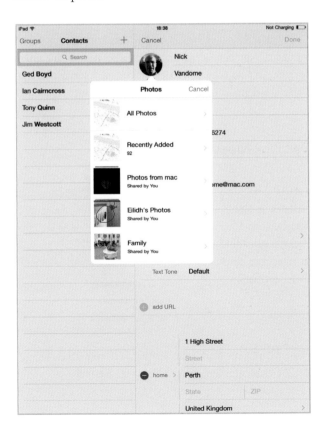

# Sharing Contact Details

You can send a contact's details to a friend using email.

**1** Open the **Contacts** app

**2** Select the contact you want to share

**3** Tap **Share Contact** underneath their details and select an option for sharing, such as **Message** or **Mail**

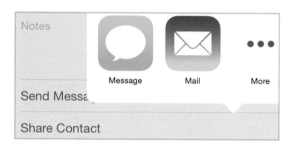

### Send an iMessage to a contact

iMessage is available on iPhone and iPad, and OS X for Mac. Using your iPad you can send an iMessage if you are connected to the internet. If you use an iPhone you can send iMessages or SMS but the iPad only has the iMessage option.

**1** Open the **Messages** app

**2** Tap the **+** button in the **To:** box and enter a contact to message and choose their email/phone number

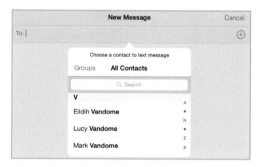

**3** Type your text and add a photo, if required, (icon to the left of the message box) then tap **Send**

# 11 Notes

Notes *on the iPad takes the place of traditional post-its. The app is simple but effective. Not only can you make and store notes on your iPad, you can also add a range of formatting options and store them in* iCloud, *so you need never forget anything again.*

# What is the Notes App?

Notes is one of the simplest and most effective of the pre-installed apps. Like several other Apple apps it also operates with iCloud. It resembles a simple, blank notepad. What you see depends on whether you hold the iPad in the portrait or landscape position.

In portrait mode (right) you can see the selected note in a floating window. The landscape mode (below) is more impressive, with a list of notes in the left-hand panel, with the current note being viewed on the right.

Don't forget

Each time a note is edited it goes back to the top of the list in the left-hand panel.

### Syncing notes

Notes can be created and stored solely on your iPad, or they can be stored in the iCloud so that they are not only backed up, but also available on other devices.

# Adding a New Note

When a new note is created it appears at the top of the list of notes, in the left-hand panel, as shown in the bottom image on the previous page. To create a new note:

**1** Tap this symbol at the upper right of the screen

**2** A new note is generated

**3** Type in your text (since the first line is used as the title of the note, enter something that tells you what the note is about on the first line)

**4** To finish, tap **iCloud** (upper left corner of the window) to take you back to the list of notes

Don't forget

If notes are enabled for iCloud (**Settings > iCloud > Notes > On**) then all new notes will be saved in the iCloud and available on any other of your iCloud-enabled Apple devices.

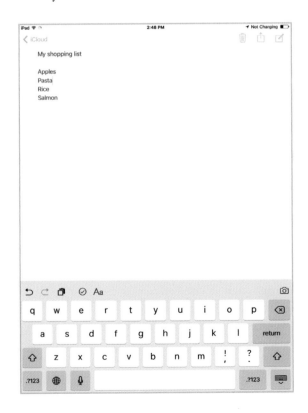

**5** Your new note will now be in the list with the date on which it was created, or updated, underneath it

# Formatting Notes

In iOS 9, the Notes app has been enhanced so that there are more formatting options than in previous versions. To apply formatting to a note:

**1** Press and hold at the beginning of the piece of text you want to format. Tap on the **Select** button

| Select | Select All | Paste | B*I*U | Indent |
|--------|-----------|-------|-------|--------|

Apples
Pasta
Rice
Salmon

tifications

**Hot tip**

Tap this button once on the Shortcuts bar to cut any selected text.

**2** Drag the yellow handles over the text you want to select

Apples
Pasta
Rice
Salmon

**3** Tap on this button to access the formatting options

**4** Tap on one of the formatting options, such as the Title, Heading or Body options for formatting the font and size, or the list options for creating a list from the selection

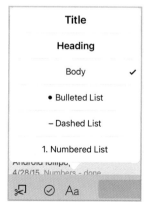

**Title**

**Heading**

Body ✓

• Bulleted List

– Dashed List

1. Numbered List

**5** The formatting is applied to the selected text (in this instance, a numbered list)

My shopping list

1. Apples
2. Pasta
3. Rice
4. Salmon

**6** Tap on this button to create a checklist from the selected text

**7** Radio buttons are added to the list (these are the round buttons to the left-hand side of the text)

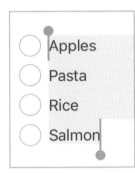

Apples

Pasta

Rice

Salmon

When using Notes on some models of iPad, there is a Scribble button which allows you to use your nails or a stylus pen to draw on the note that you are writing.

157

**8** Tap on the radio buttons to show that an item or a task has been completed

My shopping list

Apples
Pasta
Rice
Salmon

**9** Tap on this button to add a photo or a video to the note (either by taking one, or selecting from your Photo Library on your iPad)

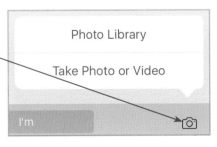

Photo Library

Take Photo or Video

# Sharing Items to Notes

In iOS 9, content can now be shared to Notes from apps such as Safari, Maps and Photos. This creates a note with a link to the appropriate app. To do this:

**1** Tap on the **Share** button in an appropriate app

**2** Tap on the **Notes** button

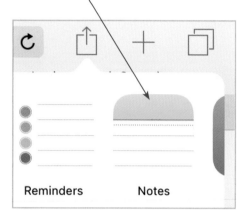

**3** The content is saved as a new note, with a link to the app from where it was shared

**4** Items such as photos and map links can also be shared to the Notes app

# (12) Maps

Maps *makes it easy to identify your location, find places, gauge traffic conditions and get directions to anywhere or from anywhere – on foot, by car and using apps for public transport.*

# What is Maps?

If you have an iPhone you will be familiar with Maps, since the iPad version is pretty similar, although much enhanced. The app shows you a map of where you are, what direction you are facing, street names, directions to a given place from where you are currently (walking, by car and by public transport), and traffic.

**The iPad version's large screen shows several views:**

- Standard

- Satellite

- 2D or 3D

To use Maps to its full potential you will need an active internet connection – either Wi-Fi or cellular.

**Beware**

To ensure that the Maps app works most effectively, it has to be enabled in Location Services so that it can use your current location (**Settings > Privacy > Location Services > Maps** and select **While Using the App** under **Allow Location Access**).

# The Maps Views

There are four views, each showing slightly different detail. Standard is probably the most useful since it shows the typical style of map layout.

Standard view – stylistic but very functional

Satellite view – as the name suggests, this is a satellite image of the area

Satellite 3D view – showing parks, water and other terrain

The different views can be accessed by tapping on the **i** symbol in the bottom right-hand corner of the screen.

Although less glitzy, the Standard view is the most practical in a lot of cases.

# Finding Places

You can find a location using a number of methods:

- Address
- By intersection
- Area
- Landmark
- Bookmark
- Contact
- ZIP/postal code

**Hot tip**

Maps has the ability to show you places of interest.

## To find a location

**1** Tap the **Search field** to show the keyboard

**2** Enter the address or other search information

**3** Tap **Search** on the keyboard

**4** A pin will drop onto the map showing the resulting location

**5** Maps will display places of interest nearby

### Zoom in and out

| Zoom in | Pinch map with thumb and forefinger and spread apart, or double-tap with one finger to zoom in |
|---|---|
| **Zoom out** | Pinch map with thumb and forefinger and bring together, or tap with two fingers to zoom out |
| **Pan and scroll** | Drag the map up, down, left or right |

# Your Current Location

## To find your current location

**1** Tap on this button

**2** A compass will show the direction you are facing

**3** Your **location** is shown as a blue marker

## The digital compass

 Compass icon – the compass is white which means it is not active

 Tap the Compass icon and it turns blue and now shows North

 Tap again and this icon points to show you the direction you are facing

Tap the compass to find out which direction you are facing. This may save you having to do a U-turn!

## Want to know more about your current location?

**1** Tap the blue **location marker** button

Current Location  >

**2** Tap the **i** symbol

**3** Details of your location will be displayed

1D Young Street

Address
**Current Location**

Popular Apps Nearby

Create New Contact

Add to Existing Contact

Report a Problem

# Marking Locations

### How to mark locations

You can drop pins onto the map for future reference:

**1** Touch and hold any location to drop a pin

**2** Touch and hold then **drag the pin** to the desired location

**3** To save it, tap the Favorites button and then tap **Add to Favorites**

**Hot tip**

Marking locations is very easy – just touch and hold your finger on the screen to drop a pin.

**164**

**4** That pin will serve as a marker for future use

**5** To see your dropped pin locations tap in the Search box and tap on the **Favorites** button

**6** A list of your dropped pins will appear

**7** Tap the one you want to view

**Hot tip**

To clear a pinned item, tap on **Edit** in Step 6 and tap on the red circle that appears next to a pinned item, then tap on the Delete button.

# Using Flyover Tour

One of the innovative features in the Maps app in iOS 9 is the Flyover Tour function. This is an animated Flyover Tour of certain locations that gives you a 3D tour of a city in Satellite view. To view a Flyover Tour:

**1** If the Flyover Tour function is available for the location you are viewing, there will be a **3D Flyover Tour** option. Tap on the **Start** button to start the Flyover Tour (from any map view)

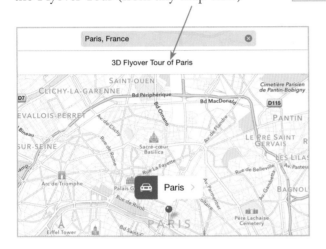

The Flyover Tour function is only available for certain cities around the world, with the majority being in the USA. There are currently over 70, with more being added gradually.

**2** The tour starts and takes you through an aerial 3D tour of the main sights of the location

When viewing maps, the compass icon in the top right-hand corner indicates the direction of North.

**3** The tour will end automatically, or you can tap on the **End Flyover Tour** button at any time

# Get Directions

Directions are available for driving, public transport, and walking:

**1** Tap **Directions**

**2** Enter the **Start** and **End** locations into the boxes at the top of the screen

**3** If the address is in the **Contacts** list tap and choose the contact

**4** Tap this icon if you want to reverse the directions

**5** Choose **Directions** for driving, or walking, or Apps for taking public transport

**Hot tip**

For some locations (such as New York and London) there are also transit options when you search for directions within the city location.

| Clear | To **Edinburgh Castle** |
| --- | --- |
| | The last section of this route requires walking. |
| Drive | Walk | Apps |

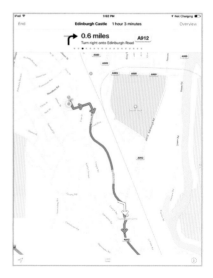

You can view the directions as an overview or a stepwise guide by tapping on the **Start** button

Alternatively, you can find directions by using a pin dropped on the map in your desired destination:

**1** Tap a **pin** on the map

**2** Tap **Directions**

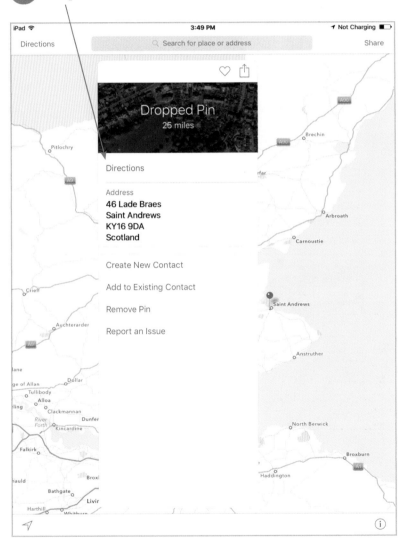

**3** **Reverse** by tapping this button

# Traffic Conditions

Maps can also show you the traffic conditions for locations.
(This feature did not work for all countries or cities at the time of
printing.)

**1** Tap the **i** symbol in the bottom right-hand corner of the
screen to view the map options, and tap on the
**Show Traffic** button

**2** The traffic conditions are shown as colors:

| | |
|---|---|
| **Green** | average speed is >50mph |
| Yellow | 25-50mph |
| **Red** | <25mph |
| **Gray** | traffic information is not available |

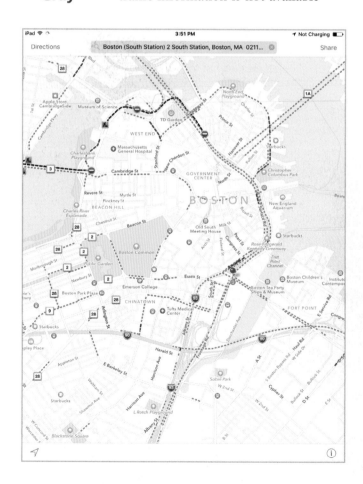

# 13 Music

*The original iPod revolutionized the way we store and listen to music and other audio content. The iPad's Music app continues this tradition and is a great music player, and now also links to Apple Music, a subscription service which provides access to the entire iTunes library of music.*

# Starting with Apple Music

Apple Music is a new service that makes the entire Apple iTunes library of music available to users. It is a subscription service, but there is a three-month free trial available. Music can be streamed over the internet or downloaded so you can listen to it when you are offline. To start with Apple Music:

**1** Tap on the **Music** app

**2** Tap on the **For You** button

**3** Tap on the **Start 3 Month Free Trial** button

> **Hot tip**
>
> To end your Apple Music subscription at any point (and to ensure you do not subscribe at the end of the free trial) open the **Settings** app. Tap on the **App and iTunes Stores** option and tap on your own **Apple ID** link (in blue). Tap on the **View Apple ID** button and under **Subscriptions**, tap on the **Manage** button. Drag the **Automatic Renewal** button to **Off**. You can then manually renew your Apple Music membership, if required, by selecting one of the **Renewal Options**.

**4** Select either an **Individual** or a **Family** membership plan (this will only start to be charged after the free trial ends)

**5** Enter your **Apple ID password** (an Apple ID is required in order to use Apple Music), then tap on the **OK** button

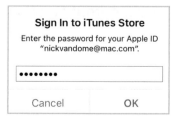

# Using Apple Music

Once you have registered for Apple Music you can begin accessing and playing the huge music resource that is available. To do this:

**1** Tap on the genres of music in which you are interested

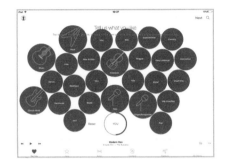

**2** Tap on the **Next** button

**3** Select specific artists, which are generated from the selections in Step 1

The selections that you make in Steps 1 and 3 are just a guide for Apple Music to start creating options for you. These can be added to at anytime by tapping on your account icon on the top toolbar and tapping on the **Choose Artists For You** option.

**4** Tap on the **Done** button Done

**5** A range of music is displayed, based on your selections in Steps 1 and 3

...cont'd

**Don't forget**

By default, music from Apple Music is stored within the iCloud and this is where it is streamed from. This means that it is played over an online Wi-Fi connection. If it is downloaded, as in Step 7, then it can be played even if you are not online.

**6** Tap on an artist or album to display it. Tap once on individual tracks to play them (via streaming)

**7** Tap here to access the menu for a track or album. Tap on the **Make Available Offline** button to download the item to your **My Music** library

**Beware**

If you do not renew your subscription once the free trial finishes, you will not be able to access any music that you have downloaded through Apple Music during the trial.

**8** Tap on the **My Music** button on the bottom toolbar

My Music

**9** The item is added to your **My Music** page and can be accessed here even if you are not online or connected directly to the Apple Music service

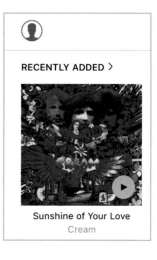

RECENTLY ADDED >

Sunshine of Your Love
Cream

## Searching for music

Within Apple Music there is a huge wealth of music, and you can search for any item and then play it, or add it to your own My Music library. To do this:

**1** Tap the Search button on the top toolbar

**2** Enter the name of an artist, group or track. The results are displayed in the search window

**3** Tap on an item to select it

**4** Tap on this button to add the item to your **My Music** library, so that it turns into a tick symbol

**5** Tap on the **My Music** button on the bottom toolbar to view the item that has just been added

Apple Music also provides access to a wide range of radio stations, including the widely advertised Beats Radio. Tap on the Radio button on the bottom toolbar to access these.

173

# Playing Music

Once music has been bought on iTunes it can be played on your iPad using the Music app. To do this:

**1** Tap on the **Music** app

**2** Tap on the **My Music** button on the bottom toolbar

**3** Select an item and tap on a track to select it and start it playing

Blondie: Greatest Hits
Blondie

**4** Tap on the middle button to pause/play a selected track. Tap once on the left-hand button to go to the previous track and the right-hand button to go to the next track

**5** Tap on this button to shuffle the order of songs

**6** Tap on the **My Music** button in the top left-hand corner to go back to your own music library

**Hot tip**

To create a Playlist of songs, tap once on the **Playlist** button, then tap once on the **New** button. Give it a name and then add songs from your Library.

**Hot tip**

Music controls including Play, Fast Forward, Rewind and Volume can also be applied in the **Control Center**, which can be accessed by swiping up from the bottom of the screen.

# iTunes Store

This is covered in more detail in Chapter Fourteen.

In the iTunes Store you can browse categories of available content which includes:

- Music
- Films
- TV programs
- Audiobooks
- Top Charts
- Genius
- Purchased (items you have purchased previously)

Use the Search box at the top of the iTunes Store window to look for specific items (in any of the iTunes categories).

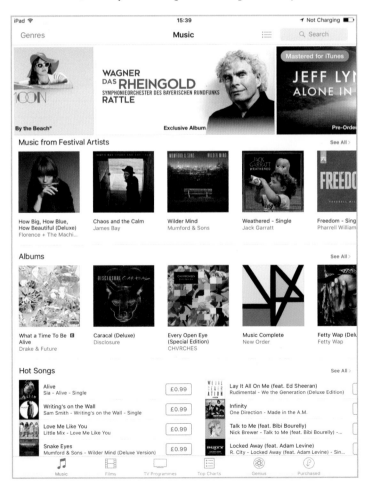

# Buying Music

Music on the iPad can be downloaded and played using the iTunes and the Music apps respectively. iTunes links to the iTunes Store, from where music, and other content, can be bought and downloaded to your iPad. To do this:

**1** Tap on the **iTunes Store** app

**2** Tap on the **Music** button on the iTunes toolbar at the bottom of the window

**3** Tap on an item to view it. Tap here to buy an album or tap on the button next to a song to buy that individual item

You need to have an Apple ID with credit or debit card details added to be able to buy music from the iTunes Store.

**4** Purchased items are included in the Music app's Library

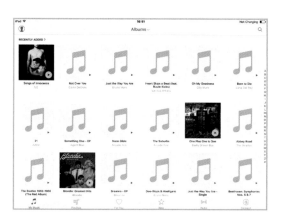

# 14  The iTunes Store

*The* iTunes Store *is a huge resource for music, movies, TV shows, audiobooks and other media.The iPad version is simple to use so you can browse the* iTunes Store *and download content quickly and easily.*

# Welcome to the iTunes Store

This app is a great hub for browsing new music, and renting or buying music and other media including:

- Songs and albums
- Videos
- TV shows and movies
- Audiobooks

There are more than 20 million music tracks and thousands of movies available for download. Purchases can be made using your Apple ID or redeeming an iTunes gift card.

You will need an Apple ID to buy things from the iTunes Store (but not view them) and for many functions on the iPad. If you haven't got one, it would be best to set one up.

**First, log in to your iTunes account with your Apple ID**

**1** Tap **Settings**

**2** Tap **iTunes and App Stores**

**3** Tap **Sign In**

**4** Enter your Apple ID **username** and **password**

**If you don't have an iTunes account with an Apple ID**

**1** Tap **Settings**

**2** Tap **iTunes and App Stores**

**3** Tap **Create New Account**

**4** Follow the instructions to lead you through the setup process

The iTunes Store has >28 million music tracks, >1 million podcasts, and >45,000 movies.

You can also create an Apple ID directly from the Apple website at https://appleid.apple.com/account

## Layout of the iTunes Store

## Finding content using Genres

An extensive range of educational material can also be accessed from the iTunes U app, which can be downloaded from the App Store.

# Music

Browse music by tapping the **Music** icon at the bottom of the iTunes Store screen.

## You can browse:

- All Genres

- Pop

- Dance

- Alternative (when viewed in landscape mode)

- More Categories

Tap on the **Genius** button at the bottom of the screen to view recommendations based on previous purchases.

Genius is a great way of finding new music.

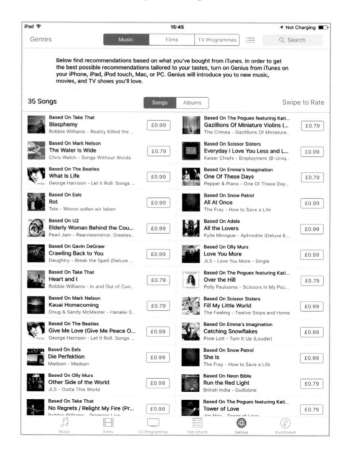

# Movies

The Store makes it easy to browse for movies and to rent or buy these. You can browse by All Genres, Action & Adventure, Classics, Comedy and More Categories.

## Previewing movie information

**1** Tap the **movie** to open an information window which shows the cost of rental or purchase

**2** Select standard definition (SD) or high definition (HD)

**3** Tap the **Trailer** image to see a short preview of the film before you buy

**4** Tap the price, and the movie will download to your iPad, if you have bought it

**5** Tap the **Share** icon to send a link to the movie by email or message, or upload to Twitter or Facebook. You can also **Gift** the movie to a friend

**Beware**

High definition versions of movies are usually more expensive to rent or buy than the standard definition versions.

# TV Shows

Just like Movies, you can buy or rent TV Shows directly from the iTunes Store.

**Browse by:**

- All Genres

- Animation

- Comedy

- Drama (when viewed in landscape mode)

- More Categories

Movies and TV shows take up more storage space on your iPad than content such as music or books.

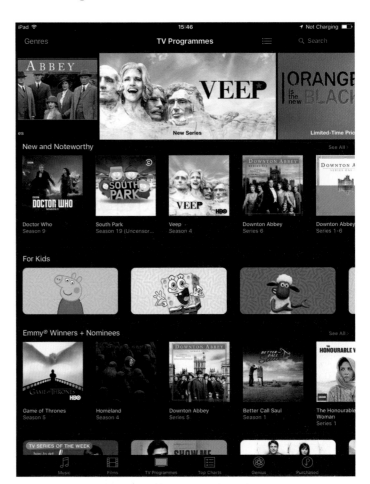

Just follow the same process as for Movies, described on page 181.

# Audiobooks

As the name suggests, audiobooks are books which are listened to rather than read. These are ideal if you have visual problems, or if you find it easier to listen to a book; for instance, if you're exercising or driving.

There are many titles available in the iTunes Store but there are many other sites listing free and paid audiobooks for downloading to your iPad:

- **http://www.audible.co.uk**

- **http://www.audiobooks.org**

- **http://librivox.org**

**Hot tip**

Enter **audiobooks** or **audio books** in the iTunes Search box at the top of the window to view the options.

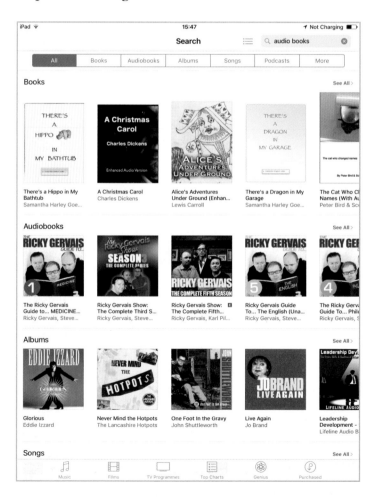

# Genius Suggestions

If you are stuck for ideas for what to buy in terms of music, films, or TV shows you can let Genius make suggestions for you. Genius will look at your previous purchases and make suggestions for you. If you have never bought a TV program using iTunes Store it will say *"You do not currently have any recommendations in this category"*.

To see the Genius suggestions, tap the Genius button at the bottom of the iTunes Store page and select a category at the top.

Above you can see items that Genius has suggested I might buy, based on previous purchases.

# 15 The App Store

*The App Store* is a vast repository of apps for the iPhone and iPad. The number of third-party apps grows by the day. You can browse and purchase from this burgeoning store right from your iPad, and increase its capabilities by adding additional functionality.

# App Store Layout

The App Store is Apple's online store, where users of iOS devices can review and download apps for almost any activity imaginable. Some apps are free, whilst others have to be paid for.

At the time of printing, over 1 billion iOS devices have been sold and there are over 1.5 million apps in the App Store, of which at least 725,000 are native to the iPad. Overall, there have been more than 100 billion downloads (all iOS apps).

With so many apps available, it is difficult to find new apps easily.

Even if you delete a previously purchased app from your iPad, you can download it again for free by tapping the **Purchased** tab at the bottom of the App Store screen. Apple will not charge you again for the app.

## What are the most popular apps?

These are Books, Games, Entertainment, Education and Utilities:

- Tap **Featured** at the bottom of the screen

- Tap **Top Charts** to see the latest apps

- Tap **Explore** to see suggestions based on your current geographical location

- Tap **Purchased** to see previously purchased apps

- Tap **Updates** to update your apps, if updates are available

# Featured Apps

The **Featured** section displays new and recommended apps. This changes frequently, so there will be a lot of new apps appearing here on a regular basis. Swipe up and down to view the available content in the Featured section.

Within the **Featured** section are various categories that can help you further refine your app search. Tap on the **See All** link to the right-hand side of each category to see more.

### Best New Apps
This shows the apps deemed to be the best new ones in the Store.

### Best New Games
This is a selection of the most popular new games apps.

### Best New Game Updates
Since games are one of the most popular items in the App Store, there is a category for updates to existing games.

### Play House
A selection of apps aimed specifically at children.

### Featured Collections
This is a selection of groups of apps covering a similar topic, e.g. fashion, nature, food, etc.

**Don't forget**

If there is a major global event taking place, such as the Olympic Games, there may an app section on the Featured page with apps relative to this event.

# Top Charts

These apps are the most popular. The screen below shows the **Top Paid** and **Top Grossing** apps on the left-hand side, and the **Free** apps on the right-hand side.

**Beware**

Do not limit yourself to just viewing the top apps. Although these are the most popular, there are also many more excellent apps within each individual category.

**Hot tip**

When search results are displayed after looking for a specific app, there is an option to view **iPad Only** apps or **iPhone Only** apps. Sometimes an app may be designed specifically for the iPhone but this can still be downloaded to the iPad.

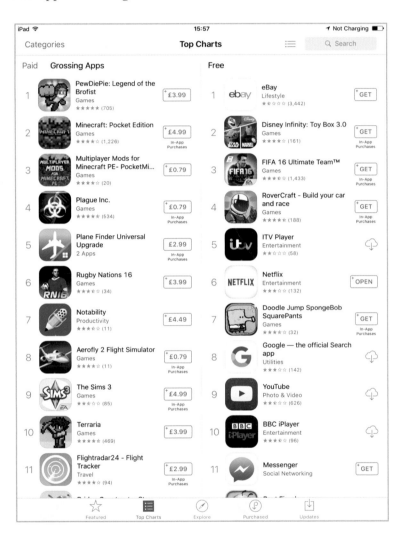

Use the **Search** box at the top of the window to look for specific apps.

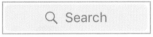

# Categories

There are currently 24 categories of apps in the App Store. This helps (slightly) to find what you're looking for, but with more than one million apps, finding an app can be quite difficult! For example, if you tap Lifestyle, you will see more than 2000 apps.

## Searching Categories

**1** Within **Top Charts,** tap on the **Categories** button to view the categories from there

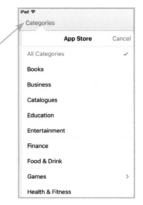

**2** Swipe down to see the full list of categories

**3** Tap on a category to view the items within it

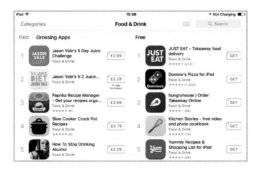

# Buying Apps

When you identify an app that you would like to use, it can be downloaded to your iPad. To do this:

**Don't forget**

Apps usually download in a few minutes or less, depending on the speed of your Wi-Fi or cellular connection.

**1** Find the app you want to download and tap on the button next to the app (this will say FREE or will have a price)

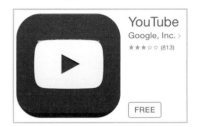

YouTube
Google, Inc. ›
★★★☆☆ (813)

FREE

**2** The button changes to show **INSTALL**. Tap on this

INSTALL

**3** Enter your Apple ID details and tap on the **OK** button

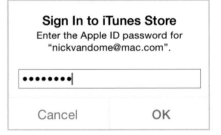

Sign In to iTunes Store
Enter the Apple ID password for "nickvandome@mac.com".

••••••••

Cancel        OK

**Beware**

Some apps have 'in-app purchases'. This is additional content that has to be paid for when it is downloaded.

**4** The app will begin to download onto your iPad

YouTube
Google, Inc. ›
★★★☆☆ (813)

**5** Once the app is downloaded, an icon is added to your Home screen. Tap on it to open and use the app

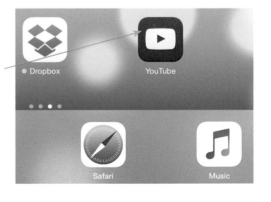

# Keeping Apps Up-To-Date

App publishers regularly update their software, ironing out bugs and making improvements. The App Store makes it very easy to see if there are any updates for the apps you have downloaded.

## How to determine whether updates are available

- You should see a red badge at the top right of the App Store icon. The number in the circle tells you how many updates you have waiting to be downloaded.

- If you don't see a badge, there may still be updates available. Open the **App Store** app, tap **Updates** and if there are any these will be listed. If none are available then you will see **All Apps Are Up To Date**.

- You can update one at a time or all at once.

- You will be asked for your Apple ID password.

- Once entered, the app updates will download in the background.

**Hot tip**

Apps can be set to install updates automatically, from within **Settings > App and iTunes Stores** and drag the **Updates** button to **On** under **Automatic Downloads**.

191

# Submitting Reviews

Reviews are quite useful since they may help you decide whether to buy an app or not.

You can submit reviews for any apps you have downloaded (free or paid).

You cannot review any app you do not own.

When you are viewing apps you can read their reviews by tapping on the **Reviews** tab, next to the description of the app.

**1** Tap the **App Store** icon to launch the app

**2** Find the app you want to review

**3** Under Ratings and Reviews you should see **Tap to Rate**

You have to download an app before you can review it.

**4** Tap on the stars to rate the app between one-five stars (you cannot give any app a zero-star rating)

**5** Tap in the main **Write a Review** section

Even if an app is total rubbish you cannot give it zero stars!

**6** Enter your text

**7** Tap **Send**

**8** You can amend the star rating before you hit the Send button

# Deleting Apps

There are several ways you can remove apps from the iPad:

- Directly using the iPad itself

- Choosing *not* to sync an app using iTunes on your computer

### Deleting directly from the iPad

**1** Press and hold an app's icon until all the icons start jiggling

**2** Tap the **X** on the top left corner of the app

**3** A box will pop up warning you that you are about to delete an app and all of its data

**4** If you still want to delete the app press **Delete**

**5** Press the **Home button** again to stop the apps jiggling

The app has gone from the iPad, but it is still on your computer.

You can resync the app back to the iPad later if you decide you would like to reinstall it back onto the iPad.

### Delete from within iTunes

**1** Connect the iPad to your computer

**2** Open **iTunes > Apps**

**3** You will see your iPad screen shown in the right panel of the iTunes Apps pane

**4** Find the app you want to delete and hover your pointer over it until an **X** appears at the top left of the app's icon

**5** Click the **X** to delete the app

The app will then be removed from your iTunes and also from your connected iPad.

Pre-installed apps (see page 26) cannot be deleted.

If you delete an app on the iPad it will remain on your computer.

# iTunes U

Although not strictly part of the App Store, the iTunes U app can be downloaded from here and used as a great educational resource. iTunes U is a distribution system for lectures, language lessons, films, audiobooks, and lots of other educational content.

## Finding educational material on iTunes U

| | |
|---|---|
| **Universities & Colleges** | Search for content by educational institution (not every university is listed at present) |
| **Beyond Campus** | Other agencies offering educational material for download |
| **K–12** | Content for Primary and Secondary education. |

## Using iTunes U

Finding content in iTunes U is very similar to using the App Store: iTunes U has a **Features** and **Top Charts** section, as well as a comprehensive search facility. Tap on the **Subscribe** button when you find a suitable course.

# Organizing Apps

When you start downloading apps you will probably soon find that you have dozens, if not hundreds of them. You can move between screens to view all of your apps by swiping left or right with one finger.

As more apps are added it can become hard to find the apps you want, particularly if you have to swipe between several screens. However, it is possible to organize apps into individual folders to make using them more manageable. To do this:

**1** Tap and hold on an app until it starts to jiggle and a white cross appears at the top-left corner

**2** Drag the app over another one

**Hot tip**

To move an app between screens, tap and hold on it until it starts to jiggle and a cross appears in the corner. Then drag it to the side of the screen. If there is space on the next screen the app will be moved there.

**Don't forget**

When new apps are downloaded, the new icon will be automatically placed at the end of the last screen.

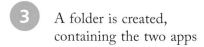

...cont'd

**3** A folder is created, containing the two apps

**4** The folder is given a default name, usually based on the category of the apps

**5** Tap on the folder name and type a new name if required

**6** Click the **Home button** once to finish creating the folder

**7** Click the **Home button** again to return to the Home screen (this is done whenever you want to return to the Home screen from an apps folder)

**8** The folder is added on the Home screen. Tap on this to access the items within it

# (16) iBooks

iBooks *is an elegant app which
lets you browse the iBooks Store
and save books and PDFs on
your bookshelf for reading later.
You can read, highlight, use the
dictionary, change the appearance
of the books, and much more.*

# The iBooks Interface

The iPad is ideal for reading electronic documents including ebooks and PDFs, and this is a key feature for many people buying the iPad. Just as Apple has made it simple to buy music and other digital content for the iPad, it has done the same with electronic books – ebooks. Browsing and purchasing is simple, and previewing books before you buy is also possible, saving you from buying books you don't want.

The iBooks app provides you with an online **Store** and also a **My Books** section to store books you have purchased or loaded yourself.

iBooks

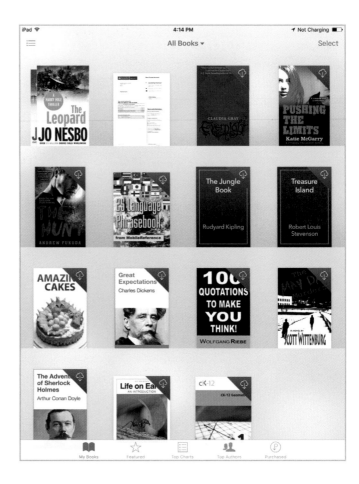

## The My Books bookshelf

- You can rearrange the books in the Library by tapping **Edit** and then tapping on books to select them

- **Move** a book to your chosen position by holding on it and dragging it to a new position

- **Delete** books by tapping on the **Delete** button and tapping **Delete This Copy** or **Delete From All Devices**

Left: You can browse your collections to see Books, PDFs, etc.

Bottom left: I have tapped **Edit** then tapped on the book which I want to delete. Tap on the **Delete** button to remove the book.

Below right: Tap on the **Move** button and select another shelf to move it to.

# Open a Book

Books (ebooks and PDFs) are stored on shelves in your Library. Just like a real library, you can browse your collection, open and read books, add bookmarks, and more.

**1** Tap **iBooks**

**2** Tap **Library** if iBooks opens on the Store page

**3** **Select a book** to read – **tap** to open

**4** Choose a specific point to start reading by sliding your finger along the thumbnails at the bottom. The current page is shown as a slightly larger thumbnail

If you close the app or book, iBooks will remember the place and the next time you open it the book will be opened at the same page as you left it.

See page 211 for details on purchasing ebooks.

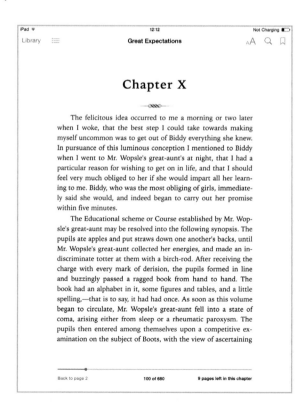

iPad 📶      12:12      Not Charging

Library  ☰     **Great Expectations**     ᴀA 🔍 🔖

### Chapter X

The felicitous idea occurred to me a morning or two later when I woke, that the best step I could take towards making myself uncommon was to get out of Biddy everything she knew. In pursuance of this luminous conception I mentioned to Biddy when I went to Mr. Wopsle's great-aunt's at night, that I had a particular reason for wishing to get on in life, and that I should feel very much obliged to her if she would impart all her learning to me. Biddy, who was the most obliging of girls, immediately said she would, and indeed began to carry out her promise within five minutes.

The Educational scheme or Course established by Mr. Wopsle's great-aunt may be resolved into the following synopsis. The pupils ate apples and put straws down one another's backs, until Mr. Wopsle's great-aunt collected her energies, and made an indiscriminate totter at them with a birch-rod. After receiving the charge with every mark of derision, the pupils formed in line and buzzingly passed a ragged book from hand to hand. The book had an alphabet in it, some figures and tables, and a little spelling,—that is to say, it had had once. As soon as this volume began to circulate, Mr. Wopsle's great-aunt fell into a state of coma, arising either from sleep or a rheumatic paroxysm. The pupils then entered among themselves upon a competitive examination on the subject of Boots, with the view of ascertaining

Back to page 2      100 of 680      9 pages left in this chapter

## Flicking through a book

**1** Tap **iBooks** to open it and **Choose a book** to read

**2** Move through the pages by **tapping the right or left margins** (moves you forward and backwards through the book). Or you can **touch and hold the bottom corner** moving your finger towards the top left

**3** Alternatively, to move to the previous page, touch and hold the left margin and slide your finger left to right across the screen

## To move to a specific page in a book

**1** Tap the **page** in the center. Controls will appear on the screen

**2** Drag the **navigator** at the bottom of the screen to the page you want

## Viewing the Table of Contents

**1** Tap the page in the center, Controls should appear

**2** Tap **Contents**

## Add a bookmark

This helps you find your place in a book (you can add multiple bookmarks).

**1** While the book is open, touch the bookmark icon, to add a new bookmark (it will turn red)

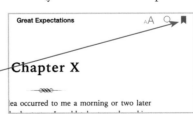

Great Expectations

Chapter X

...ea occurred to me a morning or two later

**2** Remove the bookmark later by tapping on the red bookmark icon

Hot tip

Add as many bookmarks as you want to your book – and remove them just as easily!

...cont'd

## Want the book read to you?

You will need to activate VoiceOver
(**Settings > Accessibility > VoiceOver** – see page 231).

## Highlighting text

You can use highlighters on a physical book to mark specific pieces of text, and the same can be done using an ebook:

Using VoiceOver, the iPad can read books to you (not PDFs, though).

**1** Open the page of a book

**2** Press and hold your finger on a word within the text that you want to highlight

**3** Drag the **anchor points** to include the text

**4** Choose **highlight** from the pop-up menu. Your selected text will now have a blue highlight applied

**5** To remove the highlights, tap the **text** again and then select **Remove Highlight**

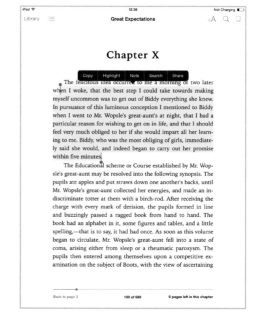

## To select an entire paragraph

Tap anywhere in the paragraph with two fingers. The whole paragraph will be selected.

# Using the Dictionary

The in-built dictionary is instantly accessible when reading your ebooks, but not within PDF files:

**1** Open the page of a book and tap and hold the **word** you want to look up in the dictionary

**2** Tap **Define** from the pop-up menu

**3** The phonetic pronunciation and definitions will appear in a pop-up box

**4** Tap the page to **close** the dictionary

Hot tip

The Dictionary is not available when reading a PDF.

# Find Occurrences of Words

You can search an entire book or document for the occurrence of a specific word:

**1** Open the page of a book

**2** Tap and hold the **word** for which you want to find occurrences

**3** Tap **Search**

A dropdown list of all pages containing that word will appear.

**Don't forget**

In the search results, tap on an occurrence of a word to view it in context in the book.

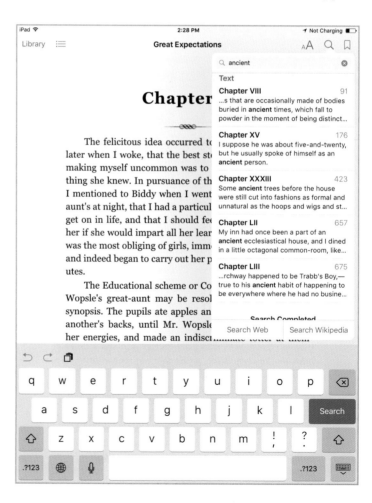

# Adjust the Screen Brightness

Depending on the ambient lighting, you may need to adjust the screen brightness. For example, if you read in a dark room you could turn the brightness down, whereas outside in sunshine you might need to turn the brightness up. To adjust the screen brightness:

**1** With the page of a book open, tap **Settings**

**2** Tap and drag the **slider** left and right to adjust the brightness

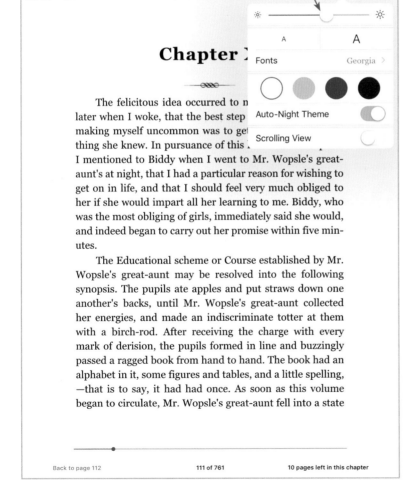

Beware

If the screen brightness is too high, it could cause headaches when reading for a long time.

# Portrait or Landscape?

The iPad adjusts the orientation of the page depending on how you hold it. If you turn it sideways, the pages rotate. This is not particularly convenient when you are lying down.

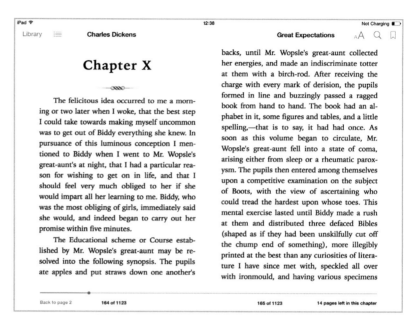

To avoid automatic rotation of the book pages:

**1** Open a book

**2** Hold the iPad in either portrait or landscape mode

**3** Swipe up from the bottom of the screen to access the Control Center

**4** Tap on this button so the screen rotation is locked

Reading a book is one of the occasions when it is definitely useful to lock the screen, especially if you are lying down!

# Using the iBooks Store

This is a great resource, containing many of the popular titles, with more being added daily. The iBooks Store is like iTunes except you buy books rather than music, and there is no rental option. Browsing the iBooks Store requires an active internet connection.

### Purchased list

This view shows all of the books you have purchased (including those titles which are free).

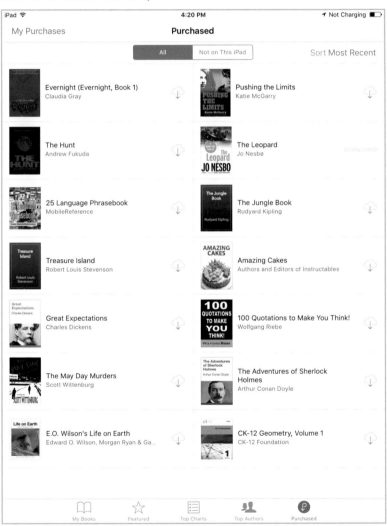

You need an Apple ID even if you want to download free books.

**...cont'd**

Browsing is made incredibly easy. You can browse by category or search for specific items.

You can search books by:

- **Featured**

- **Top Charts**

- **Top Authors**

- **Categories**

- Typing your **Search** terms into the Search box

## Sample chapters

You can't download music samples in iTunes, although you can hear 30-second audio samples before you buy. However, you *are* allowed to download short sample chapters of books before you commit to buying them. If you like the sample you will probably go back and buy the full title.

## Downloading sample chapters

**1** Open **iBooks** and find a book that you are interested in

**2** Tap the book cover to bring up the information window which floats on top of the current page

**3** Tap the **Sample** button and this will be downloaded to your library. This will usually be one or two chapters of the title

Sample chapters are available for most books so you can try before you buy.

**4** Tap the sample in your iBooks Library to open it and start reading

# Changing Fonts and Size

Sometimes the font or font size can make it difficult to read a book. With a physical book you cannot change the font, but with ebooks you can control the typeface and its size, to make the book as readable as possible.

Font too small? Don't like the typeface? Change it!

To change the font or font size:

**1** Open a book in iBooks

**2** Decide which orientation you will use to read the book – portrait or landscape

**3** Tap the **Settings** button

**4** Tap the small or large **A** to make the font smaller or larger

**5** To change the font itself, tap **Fonts**

**6** Choose from the drop-down list

**7** The book pages may have a light brown tint (sepia effect). If you like this, keep Sepia **ON** by selecting the light brown circle. If you want standard white pages, turn Sepia **OFF** by selecting the white circle

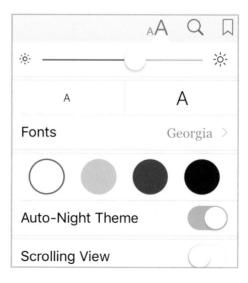

# Purchasing Books

Providing you have an Apple ID, you can download paid or free books from the iBooks Store.

**1** Open **iBooks**

**2** Tap **Store** if you are currently in Library mode

**3** Find a book you want to buy

**4** Tap its icon to bring up the floating window showing the price

**5** Tap the **gray price box**. This will turn green and will say **Buy Book**

**6** Tap **Buy Book** (if the book is free, it will say **Get Book** instead)

If you have the iBooks app on other Apple devices, such as an iPhone or a MacBook, then you will be able to read any books you have bought here too.

**7** The book will begin to download into your library and the view will change from Store → Library. You will be prompted for your **Apple ID password**

**8** Once entered, the book will download

# Find More Books by Author

If you have a favorite author, or you just want to find more books by the same author, you can:

**1** Tap the **book cover** to bring up the Information screen with a range of details about the book

**2** Tap the **Related** button

**3** You will then see any other books available on the iBooks Store by the same author

Setting up iBooks alerts is not obvious. To set up alerts go to **Settings > App and iTunes Stores** then tap **Apple ID**. Then tap **View Apple ID**. Sign in with your password and scroll down to **My Alerts**. Set up your alerts from the options shown.

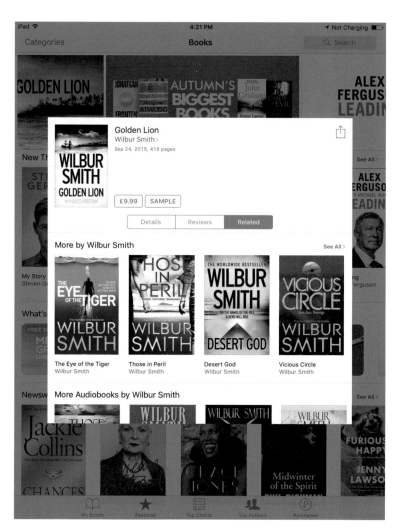

# Tell a Friend

You can let other people know about books by sending links to books which they can view on their computer:

**1** Tap on a book title to view its details

**2** Tap the **Share** icon

**3** Select one of the sharing options including messaging, emailing or sharing via a social networking site

If you see something great, share it with a friend. It's very easy to do.

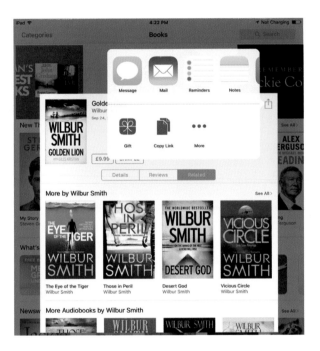

**4** Depending on the selection in Step 3, information about the item is displayed for the required person, who can then view the item in the iBooks Store, if desired

# Ebooks from Other Sources

You are not completely limited to the iBooks Store for your electronic books for the iPad:

## Epub books

**1** Download an epub book (**epubbooks.com**) on your PC or Mac

**2** Add to iTunes (drag and drop the book straight onto iTunes)

**3** Connect the iPad, then sync epub books to iPad

## Other sources for ebooks

- Smashwords (**smashwords.com**)
- Google Books (**books.google.com**)
- Kindle iPad app (**amazon.com**)
- Design your own – many programs allow you to export your files in epub format, e.g. Adobe InDesign, Storyist, Sigil, and others. Whatever software you use, if it can be saved in the epub format, you can get it onto the iPad. Another option is to save your work as a PDF, but remember: you cannot search PDFs for words, or use the dictionary. It does let you read the document easily, though.

**Don't forget**

The iBooks Store is not the only source of ebooks for the iPad. Most books in epub format will work with the iPad.

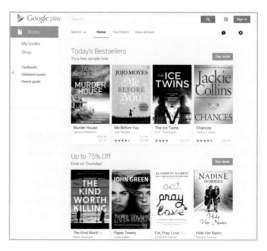

# 17 The iPad at Work

*Sadly, work gets in the way of all this play but the iPad makes giving presentations, writing documents and number-crunching fun! Instead of dragging a heavy laptop to your next meeting, try taking your iPad instead. There's not much you can't do with it!*

# Storing, Syncing and Editing

The iPad is different to a conventional computer or laptop. There is no "desktop" which means you cannot drag and drop files around and place them in folders, like you would with your laptop.

However, there are still ways of copying files to and from your iPad, allowing you to read and edit text documents, spreadsheets and presentations, and copy them back to your Mac or PC.

There are several apps available that allow you to get files onto the iPad including:

**Hot tip**

Dropbox is very useful for storing files and is available for PC, Mac, iPad, iPhone and iPod Touch (for more information see page 227). But if you want to edit the files, you will need additional software such as Documents To Go or similar. Check out the App Store.

| | |
|---|---|
| **Dropbox** | Popular on Mac and PC. Provides cloud storage which you can access from any computer. The free account gives you 2GB storage. |
| **Documents To Go and Quickoffice** | Documents To Go and Quickoffice essentially do the same thing – they let you read and edit Microsoft Office files. Both let you keep local (iPad) as well as remote (on your PC or Mac) files. |
| **iCloud** | iCloud gives you 5GB free storage. The downside is, it isn't a folder where you can drag and drop your files. Useful for keeping things in sync, though. |
| **Evernote** | Useful for storing clippings, web pages, PDFs, Word files and other documents. The free account provides 2GB storage and file types are restricted (images, audio, PDF and web pages). |

## Configure the iPad to view documents

With your iPad connected to your computer, click the **Apps** tab in iTunes. At the bottom of the screen you will see an option for **File Sharing**.

You can configure apps on the iPad to open documents on your iPad. Once you click an app, e.g. Documents To Go, a list of files readable by Documents To Go will appear. Click to select all those you want Documents To Go to open. Then click **Add...**

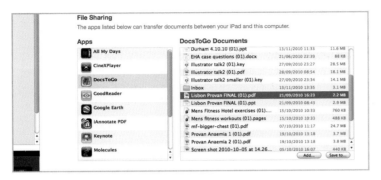

How you edit your document depends on what app you use on the iPad.

**Editing Word documents using Documents To Go**

**1** Open **Documents To Go** on the iPad

**2** Navigate to **Desktop** to add a file from your computer

**3** Choose the computer you want to connect to. Tap **My Documents To Go** to see folder contents on the computer

**4** Tap the **file** you want to edit (and save locally on the iPad)

**5** Once open, tap **Save As**

**6** Tap **Location** to select the save destination as the local storage, i.e. iPad

**7** Tap **Local Files**

**8** Tap **Select**

**9** Tap **Save**

You can now edit and save the file. In PowerPoint you can add notes and edit your slides (in Outline mode only).

Word files can be read and edited easily on the iPad.

**Beware**

If you use Dropbox to store your word processing documents you will find that although you can open them in Pages, you cannot save the changed document back to Dropbox. Annoying? However, for $5 a month you can open a DropDAV account and open and save back to Dropbox. Very easy to set up.

# Apple iWork Suite

Apple designed a suite of apps called iWork which includes a word processor (**Pages**), spreadsheet (**Numbers**), and presentation package (**Keynote**). The suite has many functions similar to Microsoft Office. All three apps are available as free downloads from the App Store (for compatible iOS 9 devices).

## Pages

1. Tap **Pages** to open

2. Select a **Document** by flicking through the list from left to right or up and down

3. Or create a new document with the **+** button

4. Select from the choice of **Templates**

5. **Edit** the text

6. Add **graphics** and then tap media – choose illustrations

7. When finished, tap **Documents** and the document will be saved

8. To **rename**, tap the name and enter your own title

9. Tap **Done**

Pages will happily open documents created in Microsoft Word and other formats, and can export in several formats including Microsoft Word.

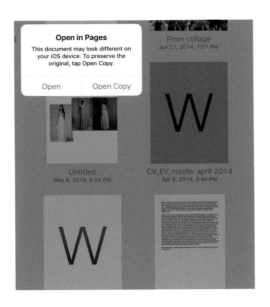

Hot tip

Pages can open and edit Word files.

Pages will import Microsoft Word files easily, though some formatting may be lost.

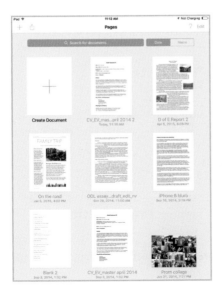

Pages shows you a window containing all documents in the Pages "folder". Swipe up or down until you find what you want.

...cont'd

### Keynote

Keynote is Apple's presentation app. It is similar to PowerPoint, although cropping and adding shapes is a bit different. Some aspects of slide design, such as cropping images and creation of shapes, are undoubtedly easier using a mouse, but simple slides can be created using the iPad.

### Open an existing presentation

**1** Tap **Keynote** to open the app

**2** Unlike Pages, Keynote only uses landscape mode

**3** Swipe left to right through existing presentations

**4** Find the one you want, then tap it to open

**5** You will see thumbnails down the left-hand side, with the slides occupying the rest of the screen

### To create a new presentation

**1** Tap the **+** button and tap on **Create Presentation**

**2** Choose a **Template**

**3** Tap **+** to add a new slide – a panel showing available master slides will appear. Select the one that suits your content

**4** Add your text

**5** **Save** by tapping **Presentations**

**6** **Name** the presentation by tapping its name and entering your own title

**7** Save to iCloud or leave locally on the iPad

**Hot tip**

Creating new presentations using Keynote on the iPad is cumbersome, and I would strongly recommend you create your presentations using a Mac. You can edit these on the iPad later if necessary.

If you save your iWork files (including Keynote) to iCloud, you will have ready access from your Mac or iOS device.

Keynote can open
PowerPoint files.

Like Pages, Keynote will open Microsoft PowerPoint files. The
presentation above was created in PowerPoint and saved before
opening in Keynote. Swipe right or left to see what presentations
are available.

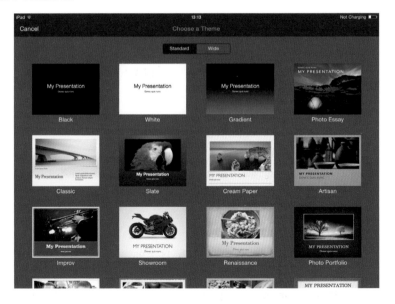

The iPad version of Keynote looks almost identical to the desktop
version. Note the thumbnails (in the top image) down the left-hand
margin with the current (highlighted) slide showing in the main
screen.

**...cont'd**

## Numbers

Numbers is similar to Microsoft Excel. Data is entered in tabular form and can be used to create all types of charts. Numbers can be used both in portrait and landscape modes.

**1** Tap **Numbers** to open the app

**2** **Enter data** into the blank spreadsheet

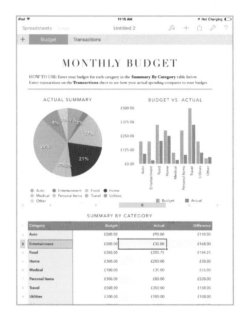

**3** Make sure you have selected the correct data type for your columns (⁴² = numeric, 🕐 = date/time, **T** = text, **≡** = calculation)

**4** Create **chart**

**5** **Save** by tapping **Spreadsheets**

**6** **Rename** by tapping its name

**7** **Save** to iCloud or locally on your iPad

# Using the iPad for Presentations

Just as you would use your laptop to present your PowerPoint or Keynote slides, you can use your iPad by hooking it up to an AV projector or screen.

You will need to buy a Lightning to VGA Adapter. This plugs into the bottom of the iPad, and the other end connects to the VGA projector.

### Present using an AV projector

 **Connect** the iPad to the projector using the Lightning to VGA Adapter

The iPad is great for giving presentations and saves you having to drag a heavy laptop around!

If you have access to an HD display you would be better using the HDMI connector (Lightning Digital AV Adapter).

 Open **Keynote**

Choose **Presentation**

The file will open in Presentation mode (rather than Edit mode).

# Editing Microsoft Office Files

You have a number of options, such as Pages, Documents To Go, Quickoffice, and a number of other apps to edit Microsoft Office files that have been created on a Mac computer.

**1**   **Connect** the iPad to your computer

**2**   In **iTunes**, go to the **Apps** tab and scroll down to **File Sharing**

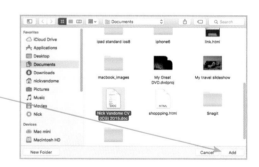

**3**   Click the **app** you want to use to edit your Office files, e.g. Pages (or Documents To Go). Click the **Add** button to add files to use with this app

**4**   Select the file you want to use on the iPad, and click on the **Add** button

This document has been opened in Pages (as a copy in Word, to ensure the original is retained in Pages) on the iPad, but could just as easily have been opened in Documents To Go.

# ...cont'd

Here is the same document opened in GoodReader, Documents To Go and Quickoffice.

In this example, the document has been opened in Documents To Go. The text is perfectly readable, and can be edited, copied and pasted.

Here the document has been opened in GoodReader (a PDF-type app like Adobe Acrobat Reader). The text can be read and copied but not edited.

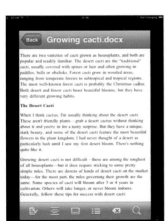

Here we have used the iPhone version of Quickoffice. The iPhone version runs just fine but the size is not optimized for the iPad screen. In order to try to fill the screen the picture has to be doubled in size, resulting in pixilation of the text.

There is also a version for the iPad called Quickoffice Pro HD.

# Get the Latest News

Because the iPad is such a great ebook reader, lots of publishers have made their content available for the web and iPad. This includes newspapers and journals. Many offer free registration, while others have limited content, with a paid subscription for full content. They are available through the App Store and can be downloaded in the same way as for apps.

**Hot tip**

The iPad is great for reading newspapers, journals, and magazines.

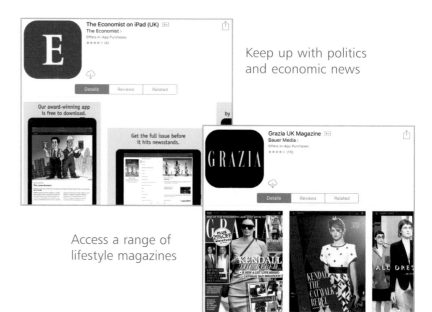

Keep up with politics and economic news

Access a range of lifestyle magazines

**NEW**

**Hot tip**

A vast range of news, current affairs and lifestyle content can also be accessed through the News app (see pages 132-134).

There are magazines for a wide variety of hobbies

For the latest in Mac news you can subscribe to Macworld and several other Mac magazines

# Organization Apps

In the App Store there is a wide range of organization apps for tasks such as note-taking. Some of these are:

- **Evernote**. As mentioned on page 216, this is one of the most popular note-taking apps. You can create individual notes and also save them into notebook folders. Evernote works across multiple devices so, if it is installed on other computers or mobile devices, you can access your notes wherever you are.

- **Popplet**. This is a note-taking app that enables you to link notes together, so you can form a mindmap-type creation. You can also include photos and draw pictures.

- **Dropbox**. This is an online service for storing and accessing files. You can upload files from your iPad and then access them from other devices, with an internet connection.

- **Bamboo Paper**. This is another note-taking app, but it allows you to do this by handwriting rather than typing. The free version comes with one notebook into which you can put your notes and the paid-for version provides another 20.

- **Errands To-Do List**. A virtual To-Do list that can help keep you organized and up-to-date. You can create your own folders for different items and have alerts remind you of important dates, events and items.

- **Notability**. Another app that utilizes handwriting for creating notes. It also accommodates word processing, and audio recording.

- **Alarmed**. An app for keeping you on time and up-to-date. It has an alarm clock, pop-up reminders and pop-up timers.

- **Grocery List**. Shopping need never be the same again with this virtual shopping list app.

- **World Calendar**. Find out Public Holiday information for 40 countries around the world.

# Printing from the iPad

The iPad can now support direct printing (called **AirPrint**).

**Hot tip**

Good news! You can print directly from the iPad. If Apple's in-built options don't work there are third-party apps which will make printing easy.

Apple has provided support for many printers, and a full list can be found at **http://support.apple.com/kb/HT4356**

## Available apps that enable iPad printing

- PrintCentral
- PrinterShare
- ePrint
- DocPrinter
- ActivePrint
- Print n Share

## Print a web page using Print n Share

1. Copy the web page URL to the clipboard

2. Open Print n Share and select **Web pages** from the options at the bottom of the screen

3. Paste the URL into the box at the top, then tap the printer icon

4. Print from the screen or from the actual web URL (the latter is probably better)

5. Choose your printer by tapping **Choose**

6. Tap **Print**

# (18) Accessibility Options

*The iPad has some very effective adjustments which make it easy to use for people with visual and other impairments. This chapter highlights the main accessibility settings which will make the iPad work for you even if you have sight or auditory issues.*

# Universal Access

Similar to the iPhone, the iPad has a variety of settings that make it easier for people with visual and hearing problems to use:

● Universal Access features

● Playback of Closed Captions

● VoiceOver screen reader

● Full-screen magnification (Zoom)

● White on Black

● Mono audio

Not all features are available for every app. Zoom, White on Black, and Mono Audio work with all apps, but VoiceOver only works with the in-built apps and some apps on the App Store.

### Use iTunes to turn Accessibility On and Off

**1** Connect your iPad to the computer

**2** Within iTunes, select **iPad** in the sidebar

**3** Click on the **Summary** pane

**4** Click **Configure Accessibility**, under **Options**

**5** Select the **features** you want to use

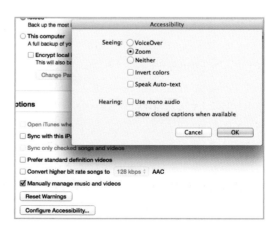

# VoiceOver

This setting enables the iPad to tell you what's on the screen, even if you cannot see the screen.

**1** Touch the screen or drag your fingers to hear the screen items described

**2** If text is selected, VoiceOver will read the text to you

## To turn VoiceOver On

**1** Go to **Settings > General > Accessibility > VoiceOver**

**2** Tap **VoiceOver** to turn On or Off

**3** Tap **Speak Hints** On or Off

## VoiceOver gestures

| | |
|---|---|
| **Tap** | Speak item |
| **Flick Left or Right** | Select next or previous item |
| **Flick Up or Down** | Depends on Rotor Control setting |
| **Two-finger Tap** | Stop speaking current selection |
| **Two-finger Flick Up** | Read all from top of screen |
| **Two-finger Flick Down** | Read all from current position |
| **Three-finger Flick Up/Down** | Scroll one page at a time |
| **Three-finger Flick Left/Right** | Next or previous page |
| **Three-finger Tap** | Speak the scroll status |
| **Four-finger Flick Up/Down** | Go to first or last element on page |
| **Four-finger Flick Left/Right** | Next or previous section |

**Hot tip**

If you cannot see the screen text, VoiceOver will read it to you.

**Beware**

VoiceOver works with the pre-installed iPad apps and some apps from the App Store, but not all of them.

# Accessibility Features

There are numerous other accessibility features that can be deployed on the iPad. These can all be accessed from **Settings > General > Accessibility**:

## Vision

The Vision options include the following:

- **VoiceOver**. (see page 231).

- **Zoom**. This can be used to increase and decrease the screen magnification. Double-tap the screen with three fingers to increase the magnification by 200%. Double-tap with three fingers again to return it to the original size. Drag with three fingers to move around the screen.

- **Invert Colors**. This setting completely inverts the iPad colors, from white on black to black on white.

- **Speak Selection**. This can be used to speak out selected text. Tap on the Speak button that appears.

- **Speak Auto-text**. Turning on this option lets the iPad speak the text corrections as you type.

The **Speak Auto-text** function (accessed from the **Speech** button in the **Vision** section) can be turned on so that auto-corrections and auto-capitalizations are automatically spoken.

Use the **Grayscale** option to remove all colors from the iPad interface. Use the **Button Shapes** option to create a background for buttons so they are more clearly defined.

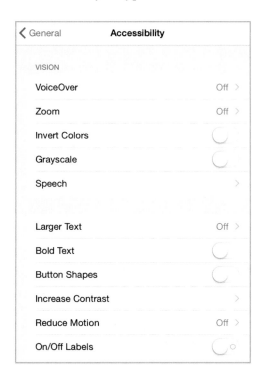

- **Larger Type**. Use this to allow compatible apps to increase the size of text.

- **Bold Text**. This can be turned on to create bold text on the iPad. It requires a restart to apply it.

- **Increase Contrast**. This aids legibility by increasing the contrast with some backgrounds.

- **Reduce Motion**. This reduces the amount of motion effects that are applied throughout the iPad.

- **On/Off Labels**. This defines the On/Off buttons further by adding labels to them as well as their standard colors.

## Hearing

The Hearing options include the following:

- **Subtitles & Captioning**. This determines the style of captions on the iPad, if used.

- **Mono Audio**. Instead of stereo sound, Mono Audio channels both right and left output into a single mono output. This is useful for people with hearing impairment, since they can hear the output from both channels in one ear. Turn Mono Audio On and Off.

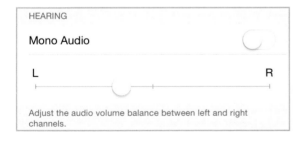

## Learning

The Learning options are:

- **Guided Access**. The Guided Access option allows for certain functionality within an app to be disabled so that individual tasks can be focused on without any other distractions. For instance, areas of a web page can be disabled so that the page being viewed cannot be moved away from.

**Don't forget**

When you first activate Guided Access for an app you will need to enter a passcode. This must also be entered when you leave Guided Access.

## ...cont'd

### Interaction

The Interaction options include the following:

● **Switch Control**. This can be used to set up your iPad for an adaptive accessory such as a mouse, keyboard or joy stick.

● **AssistiveTouch**. This contains a range of options that reduce the need for using your hands and fingers as much as for standard use.

The **AssistiveTouch** options make it easier for anyone with difficulties clicking the Home button, or using gestures.

● **Home Button** (scroll down the screen). This can be used to adjust the speed for double-clicking and triple-clicking the Home button.

### Accessibility Shortcuts

These are settings for selecting options for the functions that are activated by triple-clicking the Home button.

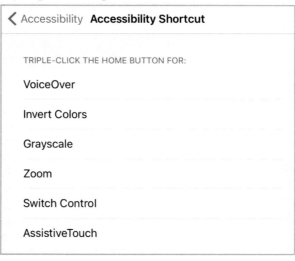

## T

## U

## V

## W

## Z